# The CDL Study
## Master Skills Guide

This ultimate handbook covers the USA and Canada in full.

# The CDL Study Master Skills Guide

## Passing The Knowledge Test, Passing The Driver's Tests, & 'How To' Handbook

This ultimate skills handbook covers the USA & Canada

MALCOLM GREEN

THE CHOIR PRESS

Copyright © 2020 Malcolm Green

All rights reserved. No part of this publication may be reproduced or transmitted in any form or by any means, electronic or mechanical including photocopying, recording or any information storage or retrieval system, without prior permission in writing from the publishers.

The right of Malcolm Green to be identified as the author of this work has been asserted by him in accordance with the Copyright, Designs and Patents Act 1988

First published in the United Kingdom in 2020 by The Choir Press

Although the author and publisher have made every effort to ensure that the information in this book was correct when published, the author and publisher do not assume and hereby disclaim any liability to any party for any loss, damage, or disruption caused by errors or omissions, whether such errors or omissions result from negligence, accident, or any other cause.

The information in this book is meant to supplement, not replace, proper driver training. Like any activity involving motor vehicles, equipment and environmental factors, there is inherent risk. The author and publisher advise readers to take full responsibility for their safety and the safety of others. Before using the skills described in this book ensure that your vehicle and all associated equipment is well maintained, and that you do not operate beyond your level of experience, aptitude and training.

ISBN 978-1-78963-145-6

**The author, with gratitude, fully acknowledges the full copyright of** the Federal Motor Carrier Safety Administration (FMCSA) **as the source of information used in part in chapter 15.**

The author, with gratitude, fully acknowledges the full copyright of the Commercial Vehicle Safety and Enforcement (CVSE) **as the source of information used in part in chapter 15.**

# Contents

| | |
|---|---|
| Preface | ix |
| **Chapter 1: CDL Skills Tests** | 1 |
| Training schools | 2 |
| CDL knowledge test | 3 |
| Practical test module 1: Pre-trip | 7 |
| Practical test module 2: Basic vehicle control/reversing and parking | 10 |
| Practical test module 3: On-road driving test | 12 |
| Example of a test | 22 |
| Conclusion | 24 |
| **Chapter 2: Mandatory Vehicle Inspection Checks** | 26 |
| Truck checklist | 29 |
| Trailer checklist | 30 |
| Things to ensure during checks | 31 |
| **Chapter 3: Coupling Procedures** | 34 |
| Semi truck coupling procedure (split) | 34 |
| Semi truck coupling procedure (close) | 36 |
| Semi truck uncoupling procedure | 37 |
| Considerations during coupling | 37 |
| Examples of bad coupling | 40 |
| **Chapter 4: Refrigerated and Curtainsider Trailers** | 42 |
| User's guide to refrigerated trailers | 42 |
| Adjustable curtain systems | 44 |
| User's guide to tautliners | 45 |
| Useful YouTube videos | 47 |

**Chapter 5: Safe Loading and Unloading**   49
   Roller cages   50
   Pump trucks   52
   Trailer height adjuster   53
   Truck height adjuster   54
   Tail lift operation   54
   Loading and unloading considerations   55
   Useful YouTube videos   56

**Chapter 6: Load Securing**   58
   The three types of load securement   58
   Securement specifications   59
   Equipment and working load limits   60
   Official load strap down and weight regulations   61
   Cross chaining, regulations and best practice for securing machinery   62
   Useful YouTube videos   64

**Chapter 7: Roping and Sheeting**   66
   The basic principles of roping and sheeting   67
   Safety notes   68
   Useful YouTube video   68

**Chapter 8: Maneuvering**   69
   Maneuvering in a spacious yard   69
   Maneuvering in a tight/small yard   70

**Chapter 9: Key Safe: Lock on Dock**   72
   Key safe (lock on dock) procedure   73
   Picking up trailers (airline lock procedure)   74
   Dropping trailers   74
   Safety notes   74

**Chapter 10: Environmentally Friendly Fuel-Saving Driving**   76

**Chapter 11: Sliding Tandem Axles**     79
  Sliding axles procedure     80
  Weight transfer     80
  Advice and safety notes     81
  Useful YouTube video     81

**Chapter 12: Sliding Fifth Wheel**     82
  Sliding fifth wheel procedure     83
  Advice     83
  Useful YouTube videos     83

**Chapter 13: User's Guide to Operating Trucks and Trailers**     85
  PTO (power take off)     86
  Roll on, roll off/hook loader     87
  Skip truck     89
  Dump truck     90
  Grab truck     92
  Container truck (sea can)     93
  Truck-mounted crane     94
  Low bed (low boy)     96
  Car transporter     98
  Drawbar combination     99

**Chapter 14: Department of Transportation (DOT)**
       **Weigh Stations**     101
  Terms used     101
  Protocol     102
  Reasons you may be asked to report     102
  Warning     103
  Advice     103

**Chapter 15: Hours of Service**     104
  Hours of service regulations: United States of America     104
  Hours of service regulations: Canada     110
  Drivers' written paper log requirements, USA and Canada     115
  Useful YouTube video     117

**Chapter 16: International Driving** — 118
   Essential daily considerations checklist — 118
   Parking — 121
   Fuel — 122
   Cold conditions: tips and dangers — 123

**Chapter 17: Tire Chains** — 125
   Fitting single chains to the lead drive axle — 125
   Fitting double chains to the lead drive axle — 126
   Advice and safety notes — 127
   Useful YouTube video — 128

**Chapter 18: Road Safety** — 129

**Chapter 19: Driver Fatigue and Falling Asleep at the Wheel** — 139
   Serious fatigue symptoms — 140
   Ways to temporarily alleviate fatigue — 140

**Chapter 20: First Aid** — 142
   Unconscious and breathing — 142
   CPR: unconscious and not breathing — 145
   Bleeding heavily — 147

A Note from the Author — 150

Gallery — 151

# Preface

This up-to-date, informative and fully illustrated guide provides all the in-depth information and support you need to aid your success in advancing from learner to pass certificate, enhance your employment opportunities and work successfully in the industry. It has been written by a class 1/AZ driver with 24 years' experience, in collaboration with a class 1/AZ trainer, and it exists for the sole purpose of helping new and returning drivers into work. Readers will find this comprehensive handbook interesting, accessible, and user-friendly.

Whether you are just starting out in your career or a returning veteran of the open road, you will find everything you need to support your next steps within these 20 chapters.

I have also included the addresses of various helpful YouTube videos as an added learning tool throughout the chapters. I highly recommend you take full advantage of these!

# Chapter 1

# CDL Skills Tests

This chapter covers all the information you need to guide you toward obtaining a full commercial driver's license. Found here in depth is information on the CDL knowledge test and the three practical test modules you will need to prepare for: the pre-trip test, basic vehicle control test and on-road driving test.

To aid learning I have made every effort to make this chapter concise as well as informative. Each topic has been simplified as much as possible.

At first look, obtaining a commercial driver's license may seem daunting. It is probably less so when it's seen simply as a series of steps. The first time you see what's involved it seems complex, but the process will become simpler every time you go over the information. That said, the amount of study and the costs involved are definitely not to be underestimated. You will need to be fully dedicated to pass all the tests!

*Note:* *This book covers all the American states and Canadian provinces/territories. The information here is tailored to all. Be aware that individual states, provinces and territories have slightly differing individual test variations, such as test duration, number of questions, pass rates etc., but all are basically the same. See the Federal Motor Carrier Safety and Administration (FMCSA) website, for the USA, or the Commercial Vehicle Safety and Enforcement (CVSE) website, for Canada, to find exact details for your area.*

### Training schools

There are two ways to obtain your CDL license:

- Undertake training at a private school and pay for it yourself.

- Approach a trucking company with its own school, and get it to put you through the training and pick up the bill.

If you decide to go through a trucking company, there are stipulations. You have to work for the company for a period of time after passing your test, and if you decide to leave early it will cost you.

Due to the costs and effort they have to invest in an individual, some companies do discriminate against drivers with bad work histories and even ask to see previous employment tax records. Some companies are very picky, some not so picky. Your history will determine how long you will have to ring around to find a company that will take you on.

*Note: Some companies also discriminate against drivers with criminal records. Parteehard Da Trucker, on YouTube, has a video offering tips for anyone with a felony thinking about getting a CDL: youtube.com/watch?v=H1kAhs-dlDw*

There are various things to take into account when you're choosing a training school. Reputation: research it. Average pass rate: what is it? Assessment drive: can you take one? Intensive courses: what do they offer? Visit them; try before you buy.

## CDL knowledge test

Passing the written CDL knowledge test is not an easy task, but it is achievable. The best way to get a pass is by dedicating yourself to the process. There are no shortcuts to this test, but there are keys: steps to take you to the summit of this particular mountain as quickly and painlessly as possible. I have endeavored here to give you as many different keys as possible.

Different types of people learn in different ways. Some are naturally academic and learn easily in a classroom; some learn better by means of being shown, others by being hands-on. Some people prefer a mix of everything.

## Using the tools and resources

To make passing the test as easy as possible, I recommend using all the resources open to you. These include:

- **CDL books.** Obtain one for your state, province or territory and read it cover to cover.
- **CDL test apps.** These can be downloaded to a smartphone or tablet and dipped into at will.
- **CDL flashcards.** These make a welcome change from books and can be carried around with you, shuffled and randomly looked at any time.
- **CDL online practice tests.** These are useful as they allow you to get used to the exam format and periodically check your progress.
- **Google.** Search for any word or term you are not yet familiar with.
- **Friends and family.** Hold question-and-answer sessions.
- **Trucking forums.** Talk to other drivers to get context and clarity about procedures you don't yet understand.

- **YouTube.** You can find multiple-choice test aids and memory improvement videos here.

## *Study advice*

Don't be daunted or stressed by this test. There are plenty of ways to make studying more effective. For example:

- Read your CDL knowledge book or app test all the way through.

- When studying, switch off the phone and lose the music. It is very difficult to study for tests properly when there are distractions around.

- Set a place and time for study sessions.

- A routine for studying is also advisable. Possibly study first thing in the morning when it's quiet and before any other distractions of the day start.

- Try picking a particular set of questions or chapters each session to get familiar with. Learn them, then move on.

- Take periodic online practice tests. These will show you where you are strong or weak.

- Keep flashcards with you of any problem questions. Dip in and out.

- Read articles connected to the topics you're working on. This helps to give another angle and change the context you're learning them in.

- Write down any questions and answers you're struggling with three or more times. Write them down in full; no abbreviations. Draw a picture; illustrate the subject you're dealing with. These are good memory techniques that work by helping to bring the questions into different formats and situations.

You may find, at least at first, that your focus will fluctuate. Don't be disheartened if sometimes while studying you feel like you're spinning your wheels and the information is just not sinking in. This happens to everyone. Bit by bit the information will link together. Try long and short study periods to see which suits you best.

## Useful YouTube videos

Take a look at these recommended videos. It's good to watch each video two or three times over a period of days. This will help the information to sink in.

- Barry Branton, "2018 CDL General Knowledge Exam Questions & Answers." youtube.com/watch?v=HOFMikRv9Bs

- Bright Side, "11 Secrets to Memorize Things Quicker Than Others." youtube.com/watch?v=mHdy1xS59xA

- Memorize Academy, "How to Memorize Fast and Easily." youtube.com/watch?v=0nFkQ4cQhME

## Practical test module 1: Pre-trip

## Classic Tractor Truck Parts Definition

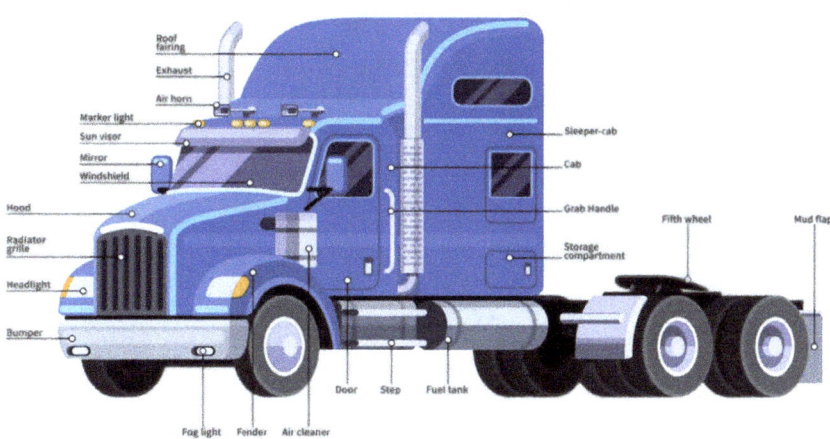

This test exists for the purposes of vehicle and road safety. The onus is on you to prove your knowledge of the workings of the vehicle to the examiner, and to demonstrate that the vehicle is free from mechanical defects and safe to drive.

There are no real shortcuts to passing this test. It's just a case of knuckling down and putting in the time to learn all the vehicle parts, operating systems, and sequences the checks are taken in. You will have to learn the whole vehicle but will only be tested on a portion of it. To pass this test you will need to learn all the components in school, study at home, and watch videos to commit the various checks to memory.

Below is an example of a vehicle pre-trip check sheet for this part of the test. You will be issued with check sheets etc. by your school.

*Vehicle pre-trip check sheet*

- Driver's door, fuel area
- Steering axle: suspension, brakes, tires
- Front of vehicle: lights, reflectors, engine
- Compartment and steering components

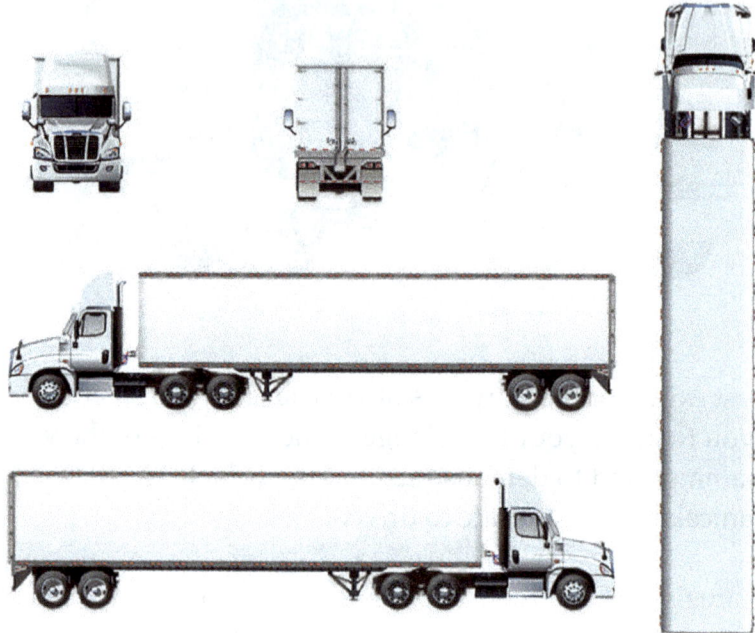

- Rear of trailer: lights, reflectors
- Under-vehicle checks: drive shaft, exhaust, frame
- Vehicle measurements
- Vehicle posture
- Fluid leaks/levels
- Wheels, wheel nuts
- Air leaks
- Drive belts, pulleys

- Drive axle(s): suspension, brakes, tires
- Coupling devices: truck, trailer
- Rear of tractor: lights, reflectors
- Trailer components: front, side lights
- Reflectors, frame
- Landing gear, tandem release
- Trailer axle(s): suspension, brakes, tires

*Useful YouTube videos*

Here is a list of very useful YouTube videos that should help clarify what this test is all about:

- Driving Academy, "How to pass the CDL Road Test." youtube.com/watch?v=2ELP7Nkv7Ko
- Apex CDL Institute, "How to perform a Class A CDL Pre-Trip Inspection." youtube.com/watch?v=EfW615ZnELE
- Smart Drive Test, "How to pass CDL Pre-Trip Inspection." youtube.com/watch?v=IsiVy0M3YSU

**Note:** *When you are ready, there are pre-trip practice tests online. Just search for one in your area.*

# Practical test module 2: Basic vehicle control/reversing and parking

You will be taught six techniques but will usually only have to execute three on the actual test.

The six techniques are:

- Straight back backing
- Offset backing to the right
- Offset backing to the left
- Parallel parking, driver's side
- Parallel parking, passenger side
- Alley docking

Usually the examiner will ask for one straight back reversing maneuver and one offset backing maneuver. The third maneuver will be one of the four remaining, but will be unknown to you in advance and is at their discretion.

Every maneuver apart from straight back backing allows you two free pull-ups (repositioning pull-forwards) and two free get-out-and-looks with no points deducted. If you decide to take extra get-out-and-looks or extra pull-ups it will cost you points, but only a minimal amount.

This is not the case if you cross a line or hit a cone during the maneuver. The mistake will cost you multiple points and may lead to a failed test.

> *Note: You have to complete all allocated maneuvers required of the vehicle and it must end up in the correct final resting position, i.e. within a certain coned-off area or with the rear of the vehicle in the correct position inside a marked-out box. If you fail to complete any maneuvers or to put the vehicle into the final resting position, you will be awarded maximum penalty points, which is a test fail.*

There are a few tips worth keeping in mind:

- Spread the vehicle out straight before starting the maneuvers.
- Pull up forward as far as you are allowed. Create as much space behind as possible. This decreases the severity of the required angles, thus making it easier to perform the maneuvers.
- If in doubt, get out! If you're not sure you can complete the maneuver, stop, get out and check. It will only cost you a minimal amount of points to do so.

### *Useful YouTube videos*

- Chick Mooney, "How To Blindside Parallel Park a Tractor Trailer." youtube.com/watch?v=VgwCkbBuZVM
- Chick Mooney, "Online CDL Training Lesson Backing Offset Right." youtube.com/watch?v=EqhfytkminA
- TN Truck Driving School, "Offset Backing." youtube.com/watch?v=B-8ndLQvq7Y

## Practical test module 3: On-road driving test

The on-road driving test can now be taken in a manual or an automatic truck.

*Note: The number of automatic trucks on the road now exceeds the number of manual trucks. Most new trucks are automatic. This means, for the first time ever, it is now no real problem to have an automatic-only license. If you select this option you will not have a problem finding work.*

Common reasons for failing the driving test include:

- Failing to show up to the test with all relevant papers: identification, license, permit etc.
- Failing to stop at a stop sign.
- Hitting or running over a curb.
- Stalling when pulling away.
- Rolling back when pulling away.
- Going through a red light.
- Hitting something.

To help you avoid these problems and more, here are some tips for your on-road driving test:

- **Take the test when you're ready and confident.** Believe in yourself.

- **Prior to test, get to know the roads immediately in the vicinity of the test center.** This makes the start and end of the test easier. Practice a lot; learn from mistakes. Build up your experience.

- **Take a pre-test mock test** if you can.

- **Know where everything is in the cab!** Familiarize yourself with all the switches: wipers, signal lights, air conditioning, heater etc. In the middle of the test it could start raining, the windows may steam up, or you could come across an accident and need to use your four ways. In these situations you do not want to be looking away from the road to search for switches. You will have to demonstrate where everything is in the in-cab inspection part of the pre-trip test, but during the inspection you will have more time and not be driving. Make sure you know where everything is so it's second nature to reach for anything needed and nothing affects your concentration on the road.

- **Try not to be distracted by the examiner.** You don't know what it is they are thinking or writing and can't do anything about it anyway. Don't be distracted from the task in hand: driving safely and within the law.

- **Select correct gear at intersections.** If you're in too low a gear when pulling out into the middle of an intersection, it will take too much time to build speed. This will impede other traffic. You will be graded on this.

- **Keep both hands on the steering wheel.** Keep hands on the wheel at all times unless you are shifting gears, signaling etc. You need to be in full control of the vehicle at all times. It seems simple, but people do forget this rule and get points deducted.

- **Straying from your lane:** drifting across the lane into other traffic is obviously a danger to others and shows lack of control of the vehicle.

- **Changing lanes:** avoid turning off your turn signal until the entire truck and trailer are all the way into the new lane. You need to indicate your full intention during the maneuver, avoiding other vehicles becoming confused and trying to pass you.

- **Take notice of truck-specific road signs.** These signs are set out at strategic points on the road to give information or warnings on situations ahead, such as restricted routes, bridge heights, weight limits etc. At a certain point during the test, after you've passed a road sign or a truck-specific sign, the examiner will ask you what information was on it. If you do not know the answer, this will be looked upon as lack of observation and poor road safety, and you will be marked down.

- **Stop clearly behind the stop line at intersections.** This is very important. Being too far forward is seen as a hazard, displaying a lack of observation and impeding other road users.

- **Check your mirrors constantly.** Ideally check the mirrors every five to ten seconds. You need to show observation and check the road conditions before making a maneuver. Check the position you are in relative to other vehicles and know what other vehicles are doing. Be aware at all times of exactly where the back of the truck or trailer is and of any cyclists, motorcyclists, emergency vehicles etc. Make sure to move your head slightly while checking the mirrors to make the examiner fully aware that you're doing so.

- **Gear shifting in the middle of an intersection:** avoid doing so when crossing a railway track or during tight turns. It takes one hand off the wheel and affects concentration during the maneuver.

- **Avoid shifting on a downhill incline.** If you have to go down a steep grade you should be in the correct gear from the start. There is less risk of losing control of the vehicle or having to rely on and overwork the brakes.

- **Turning from a double lane:** when doing so, be sure to position your truck in the outside lane and turn from there. If you turn from the inside lane you may not be able to complete the maneuver.

- **Observe and obey speed signs.** If safe to do so, increase or decrease speed in accordance with road speed signs.

The examiners are often from police or military backgrounds. These people take dangerous vehicles and their personal role in public safety very seriously. To gain their confidence, you will need to demonstrate the following:

- **Competence:** ability to keep the vehicle fully under control at all times.

- **Anticipation:** forward thinking, awareness of all road users and of possible hazards ahead of time.

- **Road positioning:** choosing the correct lane at the correct time and taking up two where necessary.

Your attitude is important. The examiners are looking for a driver who is level-headed, positive, responsible and confident.

*Note: Ex-forces people often mix socially with people of similar experience and not more alternative types. Due to negative media stereotyping, an unconscious misunderstanding of more alternative people is possible.*

*With this in mind, if you are alternative-looking, it may be worth considering being a bit conformist for a few hours. Doing what is necessary not to stand out may help you to gain respect and avoid being misunderstood. One thing is for sure: they will not change for you.*

*Bad habits*

To pass the road test you will have to drive in a certain way adhering to all the rules of the road, demonstrating a strong ability to concentrate and a high level of control over the vehicle.

Bad habits built up over time can easily be your undoing on the test day. They don't just disappear overnight. Either get rid of them or be aware of which ones prevail and could be your Achilles heel on the day.

The usual culprits are:

- Poor road positioning.
- Erratic steering and braking.
- Incorrect road speed.
- Missing information on signs.
- Forgetting to signal at an intersection.

- Cancelling signal too early.
- Tailgating other vehicles.
- Pulling away from the curb without checking blind spot.
- Lack of anticipation.
- Lack of checking the mirrors.

Make a concerted effort to practice away the old habits. During the few weeks leading up to the test, drive your car or truck as if it's test day. Make driving to the rules second nature. Not having to worry about making mistakes due to bad habits will free up more headspace and concentration for all the other necessary details of the exercise.

*Note: If you have a car, fold up the interior mirror and use side mirrors only.*

## The day of the test

Most people get nervous. On the day of the test try to keep to your normal routine. Eat breakfast. If you find you're feeling butterflies in your stomach, try to eat something anyway. This will help to keep your energy levels up, as nervousness tends to burn up a lot of energy. Ideally you don't want to be even more stressed by feeling hungry.

Prepare your day with no rushing around. Plan to have a calm day but stay occupied.

It can be helpful to ease nerves by drawing confidence from experience. Remember all the preparation you've put in leading up to now. All the effort, the hours spent in the truck and the on-road experience you have gained.

It's also a good idea to take a 45-minute pre-test lesson. Talk to the instructor, refamiliarize yourself with the truck, get into the driving zone.

If possible, arrive at the test center in plenty of time. Give yourself ten minutes to relax. Take five or ten good long deep breaths. This will help circulation and help get oxygen to the brain.

If you find yourself with an overactive chattering mind, answer it with positivity, using the knowledge you've gained up to now as an edge. Say to yourself, "I'm used to focusing, I've put plenty of practice time in, I've got experience, I can do this," etc.

Switch off your phone, then head into the test center, ideally five to ten minutes prior to the test. Show proof of identity etc.

Start the test confidently and steadily. Once you get going, focus will concentrate the mind and help to ease nerves.

In case your throat gets dry, having a bottle of water with you is a good idea.

Out on the road, traffic conditions are unpredictable. You never know what's around the next corner or at the next intersection. During the test there will be certain situations that you can expect and shouldn't find surprising. Examples of these are people walking out into the road from a bus at a busy bus stop, or the traffic signal light sequence at a road junction. If the light's been green for a while, it's a safe bet that it's going to change soon.

Show caution on approaching pedestrian crossings. If there's a crowd of people, anticipate what might happen next and keep planning ahead. It's likely that someone will have pressed the button; it's just a matter of time until the light changes. It's important to take care and be observant, particularly if the crossing is close to an awkward intersection or partially obscured by a large vehicle. Keep scanning the area for people who may not be paying attention, whether they're in a hurry or on their phones, and for distracted children who may obliviously step straight out into the road.

Be fully aware of all other traffic. Effective observations are very important in avoiding potential incidents and accidents. Plan ahead and expect the unexpected. If you can't see around a corner then approach it slowly, ready for any possible hazards. At an intersection where you can't see very well, emerge carefully, observe properly and don't assume the road ahead is clear. In fact, it's better to always expect the worst.

Take in all the information around you, and keep planning and scanning. Be aware of cyclists or motorcyclists preparing to pass on the inside or outside, and emergency vehicles speeding by. Don't forget to keep checking the mirrors (and being seen to check them), and also keep checking the blind spot when pulling out or changing lanes.

Try to be prepared for what's next at all times. When meeting oncoming traffic on narrow roads, think about not only the space you're going to pull into but also the room you're going to need to pull out unhindered. Consider what parked lorries unloading on the side of the road could be obscuring from your view. Take note of parked vehicles or traffic lights in the distance, and think about what's after the vehicles and traffic lights. If you do not turn into a narrow road steadily, exercising caution, but instead keep on heading into the middle of the road, expecting the road to be clear, you could run into trouble and possibly have to take evasive action. Keep up your awareness and look out for any potentially dangerous situations.

In the appropriate situations, try asking yourself, "Can I enter and exit the box junction before the lights change?" "Have any of the people at the pedestrian crossing pressed the button?" "Is it safe to go around the stopped bus or are there people starting to cross?" It is very important to keep anticipating and planning. If you fail to keep doing this, it is more than likely that mistakes will start to happen.

Remember, signs and road markings are there to help you. Look well ahead and try to spot signs early so that you have time to think and react. Be aware of dual lanes, bus lanes or cycle lanes ending, all of which result in traffic merging. All it takes is missing the signs and road markings and you could end up being in the wrong lane, driving the wrong way up a one-way street, or going over the speed limit. If you don't notice when the speed limit rises and it's safe to drive faster, you could even end up driving too slowly. Examiners will mark down a driver for failing to increase or decrease speed according to signs and road conditions.

Avoid assumptions. Don't assume that the speed limit on the road you are driving on is not going to change, that the road will continue as two lanes, or that you can't drive in any bus lanes or two-in-one lanes.

Never assume you have failed your test. If you make a mistake that puts you off, such as being in the wrong gear when moving off, don't continue on the test dwelling on what has just happened. If you do, you will not be concentrating in the moment and may start to make more and more mistakes. Just let go of the past situation, recover from it and focus on what's next. Keep going. Be positive.

Whatever you do, try not to go through the whole test and then fail on any test questions at the end! Examiners see this knowledge as an equally important part of the test.

*How to stack the odds in your favor: the short version*

- Choose the best driving school.
- Practice, practice, practice.
- Keep the same vehicle.
- Learn the route.
- Learn the roads around the test center.
- Know the difficult corners and intersections.
- Overcome bad habits.
- Anticipate; think ahead.
- Avoid lack of road progress.
- Avoid hesitancy; keep the wheels rolling.
- Be aware at all times.
- Focus.
- Check your mirrors constantly.

## Useful YouTube videos

Steve McIntosh. "Test your Class A CDL Road Skills – Ride Along." youtube.com/watch?v=wvWgTJve6-s

Todd Anderson, "Knight Transportation Road Test." youtube.com/watch?v=A6eIpXurkEE

## Example of a test

I have included this section on my test experience for information purposes only. It's not an exercise in tutoring or self-indulgence. My hope is simply that including this might help in what I know is a very tough, expensive and vital challenge when trying to get into this industry.

I took an intensive five-day training course. The trainer was ex-military and used a stick to jab me in the ribs if I made a mistake. The idea being, if I was about to make the same mistake, I would connect it with those jabs and remember. I would say this technique worked.

I knuckled down and focused hard. The first three days really went well and my confidence grew. That was until the mock test on the fourth day. That day I couldn't do anything right. I bounced off curbs, pulled out on cars at junctions, and messed up on the reversing. My confidence started to crash. The instructor was a good man and he told me that during his career he'd seen this happen many times before. It was just the mind letting go for a day after intensive focusing for long periods, and my concentration would return.

On the day of the test itself, I had had a very poor night's sleep and was tired. Knowing that I would need to be fully awake and alert, I had a very strong coffee prior to the test. It didn't help my nerves but did do the trick. Fortunately on the pre-drive lesson to the test center I found that my focus had fully returned.

*Note: In my experience coffee did help with alertness, but I wouldn't recommend it to a non-coffee drinker.*

During the day I incurred four main problems on the drive:

- **Focus.** My trainer had taught me to check the mirrors every seven seconds, actually turning my head slightly to demonstrate to the examiner that I was doing so. This necessary but constant distraction made concentrating on all other aspects of the test very difficult indeed. To aid focus, I pushed myself to get into the zone. I told myself to think only about the test itself and dismiss all thoughts of the past or future. "Pass or fail, money no money, I'll worry about all that when I've finished." Some thoughts did arise and I just ignored them.

- **Hesitancy.** On approaching a busy junction with oncoming traffic, I couldn't assess whether the gaps between vehicles were quite big enough for me to be able to pull out. If I'd obstructed another vehicle or caused it to slow down and alter its course, the most likely outcome would have been an instant fail. However, erring on the side of caution and trying to keep the truck wheels rolling, potentially using up some hesitancy points, would be at least a possible pass if the rest of the drive went well.

- **Random chance.** I encountered a group of schoolchildren who, on seeing me coming, decided it would be a good idea to wind me up by wandering in and out of the road in front of the truck. They continued to do this for at least a minute or two. By this time my blood pressure was going through the roof. *While I realize the children are our future........., at that moment all I wanted to do was put my size 10 boots right up their arses.* ☺

- **Sudden stop.** At one point on the route, I saw a few people waiting at a crossing a short distance ahead. I didn't know if they had pushed the button; all I knew was that the lights were showing no sign of changing. The road ahead of me was clear, but I had to make a decision to accelerate or just go on very steadily. My decision was to just crawl up to the lights. Just as I arrived the lights suddenly changed to red. Even at this low speed, I had to stop sharply. At that moment the examiner slammed his clipboard down hard onto the dashboard, as if to make out I'd almost sent him through the windshield. This didn't do my nerves much good!

Knowing most of the route was a big key. Because I knew most of the roads, the constant mirror checking wasn't as big an issue as it could have been. It was also an advantage to know in advance about speed limits, tight turns, awkward obstacles, traffic light systems, steep hills, narrow roads etc. However, some aspects, such as the experience with the kids, were completely out of my control.

I was very fortunate that on the day things went my way.

> *Note:* As of February 2020, new entry level training core classroom curriculum and behind the wheel (BTH) driving requirements came in to affect. See FMCSA/ CVSE websites for full details.

## Conclusion

I fully understand how difficult, time-consuming and expensive it is to gain a class 1/AZ license. I also understand that everyone is different. What works for one person may not work for another. I recommend you cherry-pick from the information provided, based on whatever works best for you. I hope this chapter helps with the challenge of passing your tests.

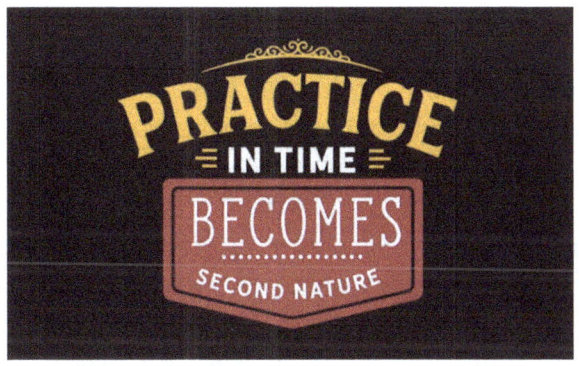

# Chapter 2

# Mandatory Vehicle Inspection Checks

This chapter outlines the mandatory vehicle checks which you, as the driver, must carry out. I have also included examples of paperwork and checklists likely to be given to you to fill in. These are largely self-explanatory, but you do need to be thorough before signing any paperwork, as you could find yourself blamed for any damage or defects that you've overlooked. It can also threaten your license if any defects are discovered by the police or DOT inspectors out on the open road.

This paperwork is legally binding, so be sure not to rush and only sign it if you're confident that you have been diligent in your checks.

*Note: If you are rushed, disturbed or distracted while completing these checks, or the paperwork, it's advisable to retrace previous steps taken before continuing. Remember, at the point of signing the vehicle becomes the driver's responsibility. If it's not roadworthy, don't sign and don't take it out on the road.*

A couple of points to remember:

- Raise suspension to gain access to inspect the inner of a set of dual tires.

- Always keep the windshield washer bottle at least half-full. Failure to do so could result in a roadside fine.

## Vehicle Checks

### Cab Front

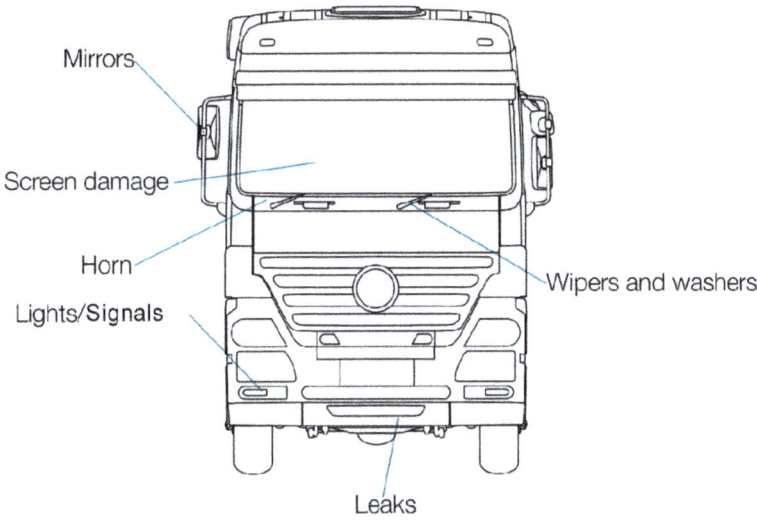

Mirrors
Screen damage
Horn
Lights/Signals
Wipers and washers
Leaks

### Cab Back

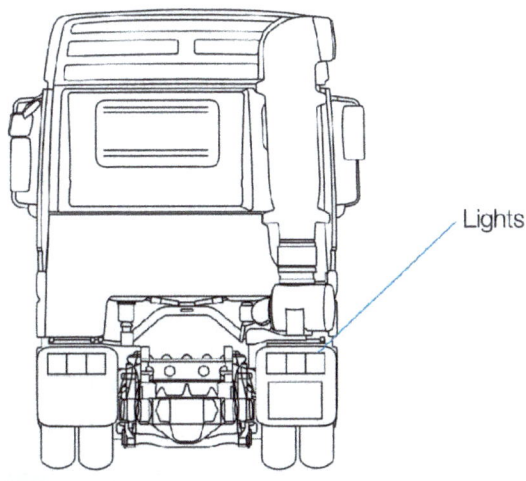

Lights

# Vehicle Checks 2

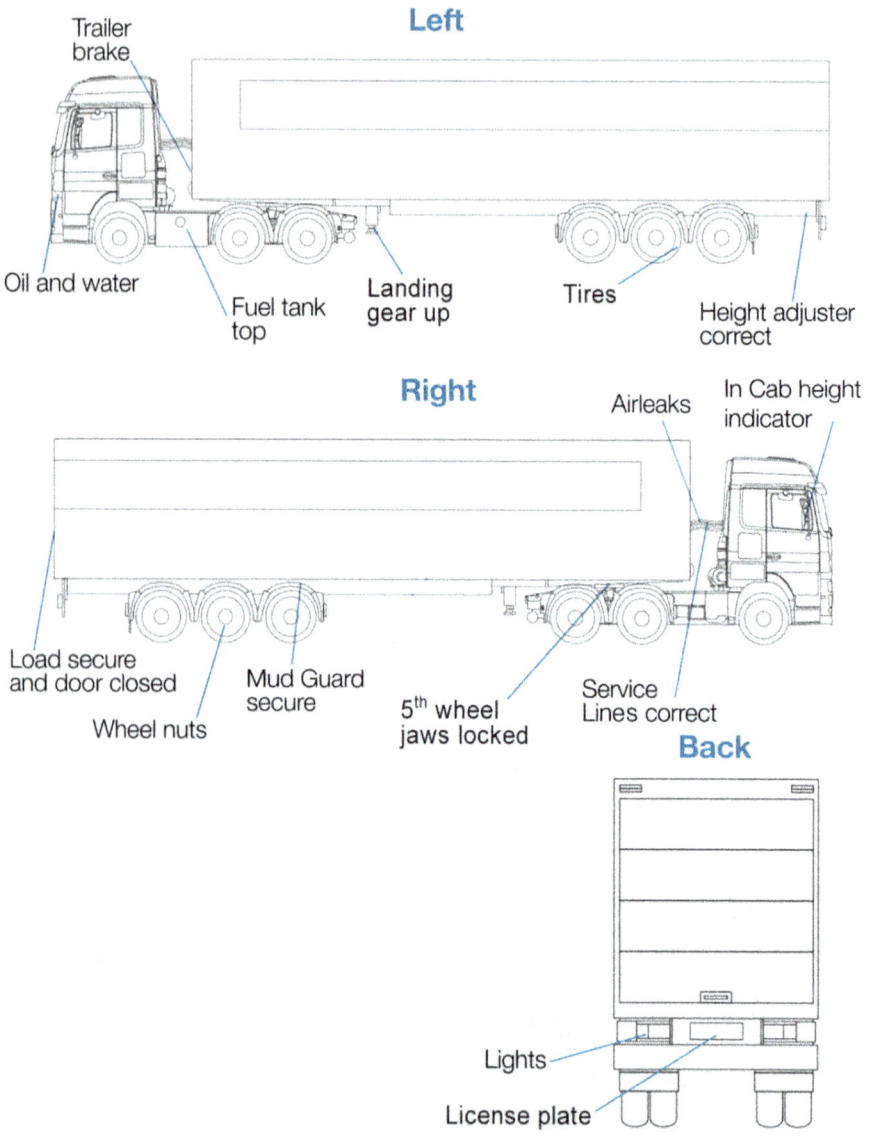

## Truck checklist

Fill each box with a check mark if the condition is satisfactory or a cross if there is a defect.

| TRUCK CHECK | JOURNEY | |
| --- | --- | --- |
| | BEFORE | AFTER |
| Air compressor, air lines | | |
| Battery | | |
| Defroster, heater | | |
| Brakes, parking brakes, service, brake accessories | | |
| Coupling devices | | |
| Belts, hoses | | |
| Drive line | | |
| Exhaust | | |
| Fifth wheel | | |
| Fluid levels, leaks | | |
| Axles, suspension system | | |
| Tires, wheels | | |
| Mirrors | | |
| Lights: head – stop, tail – dash, turn indicators | | |
| Fuel tanks | | |
| Steering | | |
| Safety equipment: fire extinguisher, flags, flares, reflective triangles, spare bulbs and fuses | | |
| Transmission, clutch | | |
| Screen | | |
| Wipers and washers | | |

## Trailer checklist

Fill each box with a check mark if the condition is satisfactory or a cross if there is a defect.

| TRUCK CHECK | JOURNEY | |
| --- | --- | --- |
| | BEFORE | AFTER |
| Brake connections | | |
| Brakes | | |
| Coupling devices | | |
| Tires: inflation, tread depth, damage | | |
| Wheels: satisfactory and secure | | |
| Wings, mudguards and spray suppression equipment: satisfactory condition and secure | | |
| Signals: in good working order | | |
| Landing gear | | |
| Marker boards: satisfactory condition, free from damage | | |
| Lights: in good working order, free from damage | | |
| Doors, roof | | |
| Load security restraints in place: bars/straps at rear | | |
| Straps, tarpaulins | | |
| License plate: satisfactory condition and secure | | |
| Park brake operational/air leaks: audible check | | |

## Things to ensure during checks

*Truck*

- Steering: no juddering or excessive noise.
- Foot brake: working, no air leaks.
- Windshield: satisfactory, no cracks or large chips.
- Mirrors: no cracks.
- Wipers: functioning, no peeling rubber.
- Oil and water: correct level.
- Windshield washer bottle: at least half full.
- DEF: additive level, cap tight, no leaks.
- All lights including fogs: working, no lens cracks, clean.
- Suspension: set to correct level, no air leaks.
- Fuel: level, cap tight, no leaks.
- Tires: adequate tread depth; no uneven wear, punctures, splits or gashes.
- Wheel nuts: tight. Check visually and try at least three per wheel by hand.
- Fifth wheel: visually check jaws locked and dog clip in place.
- Fenders: no holes, secure.
- Air lines: no leaks, free from damage, correct length for travel.
- Service lines: free from damage, correct length for travel.
- License plate: no cracks.

*Trailer*

- Landing gear: lifted to correct height, handle stowed securely.
- Suspension: no leaks, height adjuster set at correct travelling height.
- Tires: adequate tread; no punctures, splits or gashes.
- Marker lights: all working, clean.
- Tail lights: all working, clean.
- Load: secure, correct load.
- Back doors: secure, locking mechanism located properly top and bottom.
- License plate: correct for vehicle, secure.
- If refrigerated, check: underslung fuel tank cap rubber seal intact, fuel gauge level.
- If tail lift, check: secure, no hydraulic leaks, all necessary cables present.

Some drivers prefer to take a "belt and braces" approach. They start at the front of the vehicle and work their way around, doing major safety checks first: fifth wheel jaws locked, dog clip in, air lines, service lines, tires, wheel nuts, back doors, any obvious defects or damage, etc. Then they go back and start again, checking all other details as they go. The idea is that any major checks missed first time round should be picked up on the second walk round.

*Note:* *Any defects and/or damage, such as dents, scratches, and scrapes, should be recorded in writing on company paperwork supplied or drawn on images supplied.*

Newer trucks have a fitted dashboard screen which indicates and monitors most systems on the vehicle: oil, water, lights, suspension height, driving time etc.

# Chapter 3

# Coupling Procedures

This chapter deals with coupling and uncoupling. The diagrams show some of the problems that can be encountered if you are not on your game.

Coupling and uncoupling are reasonably straightforward procedures, but make sure that you do not let time constraints pressure you into being rushed or distracted. This is where mistakes happen! Take enough time to carry out  the task properly. If you do get distracted by someone or something, make sure to **retrace** previous steps taken before proceeding further.

## Semi truck coupling procedure (split)

1. Reverse up to the trailer, then put park brake on. Check trailer brake is on and fifth wheel bar (handle) pulled out. Is the trailer height correct?
2. Check the trailer skid plate, kingpin, turntable jaws, airlines, leads and connections for any damage.
3. Adjust tractor to the correct height. Height of the tractor's turntable (fifth wheel) should be slightly higher than the trailer skid plate.
4. Block trailer wheels.
5. Connect service lines and airline.
6. Reverse under until pin locks in.
7. Select first gear and tug trailer twice, making sure trailer is properly locked onto the tractor.
8. Park brake on.
9. Visually check fifth wheel kingpin jaws are locked in.
10. Trailer brake off.
11. Wind up legs.
12. Fit license plate.

*Note: Some companies do not allow split coupling. Always check with the company transport office.*

During split coupling, always, always **check the trailer brake is on**! Once you fit the airline the brakes could automatically release. If the brake is not on and the yard is on an incline, there is an extreme **danger** of the trailer rolling away, or rolling forward and crushing you against the back of the cab.

## Semi truck coupling procedure (close)

1. Reverse up to trailer, then put park brake on. Check trailer brake is on and fifth wheel bar pulled out. Is the trailer height correct? (If MAVIS rail fitted, slide it all the way across.) Check the trailer skid plate, kingpin, turntable jaws, airlines, leads for any damage.

2. Adjust the tractor to the correct height. The height of the tractor's turntable (fifth wheel) should be slightly higher than the trailer skid plate.

3. Block trailer wheels.

4. Reverse under the trailer until the pin locks in.

5. Select first gear and tug trailer twice, making sure trailer is properly locked onto the tractor.

6. Park brake on.

7. Visually check fifth wheel kingpin jaws are locked in.

8. Fit service lines/airlines.

9. Trailer brake off.

10. Wind up legs.
11. Fit license plate.

*Useful YouTube video*

J-Tech, "Coupling and Uncoupling Tutorial."
youtube.com/watch?v=VPJ1biinnx8

## Semi truck uncoupling procedure

1. Find level solid ground.
2. Park brake on.
3. Ensure trailer brake fitted on trailer is in the on position.
4. Block trailer wheels (ideally front axle in case trailer legs sink, thus lifting rear axle(s) off the floor).
5. Wind legs down.
6. Service lines/airlines disconnected.
7. Remove license plate.
8. Pull fifth wheel locking lever out (unlocked position).
9. Double-check all procedures.
10. Drive out.

*Note: If the ground is soft, put a large wooden block or blocks under the legs to stop them sinking into the ground.*

## Considerations during coupling

Make sure the trailer is at the correct height. If the height is incorrect, you can use the handheld suspension unit on a modern high-tech tractor to raise or lower the truck to match the trailer height. Alternatively, the tractor may be fitted with a fifth wheel raise/lower option. If neither option applies and the trailer is empty, it may be possible to at least lower it using the landing gear winding handle.

*Height adjuster*

*Landing gear/legs*

The object of the tug test is to ensure that the fifth wheel kingpin is locked in. Give the trailer two strong tugs, but do not drag it forward as this will risk damage to the landing gear legs etc.

## MAVIS rail

The name "MAVIS" is short for "Montracon Articulated Vehicle Interconnection System." A MAVIS rail is a piece of modern technology fitted on some newer trailers. It is located on the bulkhead (front of trailer). It allows the service lines and airlines to be connected from the ground without having to climb onto the back of the truck. Pull one or two levers (pins) and the whole rail slides out. Be very **careful** of other traffic while using it, as you will have your back to any possible danger, and make sure to lock it back into its original position when you are finished.

*Suspension airbags lowered too far*

*Suspension airbags raised too high*

*Turn table/release handle & dog clip*

*Sliding MAVIS rail*

## Examples of bad coupling

Bad coupling example A shows a trailer which is too high, therefore missing the pin. This will result in damage to the rear of the cab and to the trailer bulkhead.

Bad coupling example B shows a trailer which is too low. This will cause damage to rear lights and mudguards.

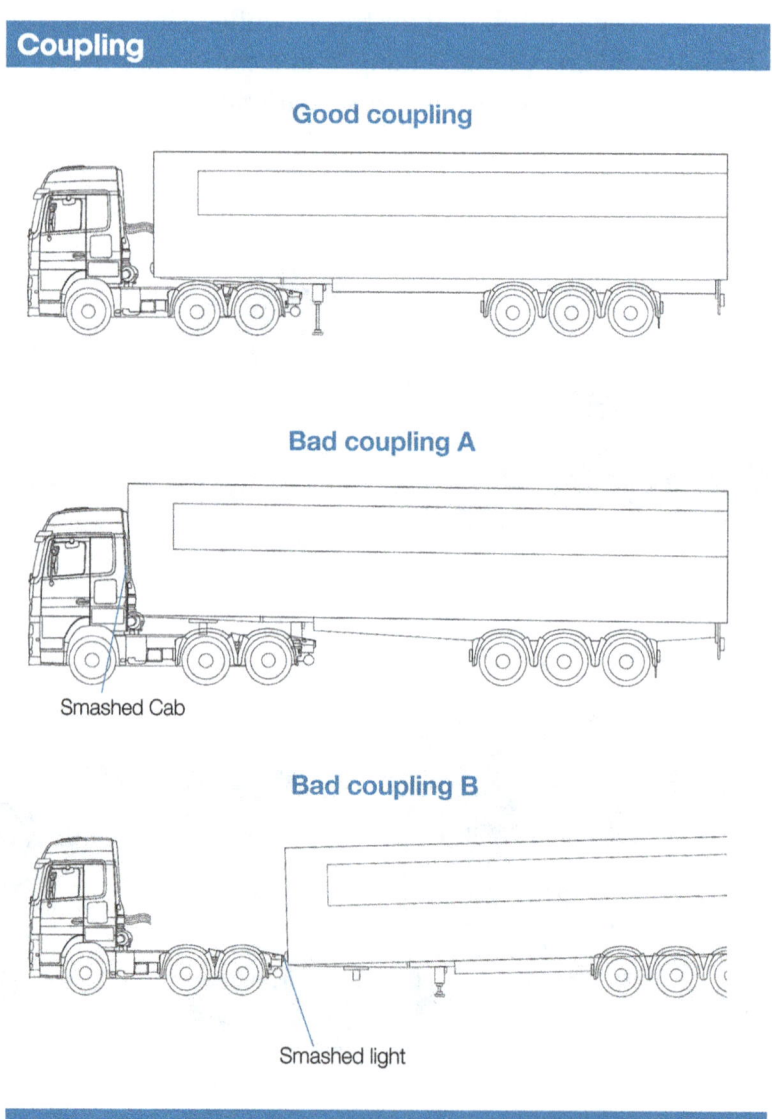

# Chapter 4

# Refrigerated and Curtainsider Trailers

This chapter contains a thorough guide to using two of the most commonly used trailers: refrigerated trailers (reefers) and curtainsider trailers (tautliners). The same or very similar steps also apply to straight rigid trucks. Technology on trucks is ever-changing; however, all are basically similar to operate.

## User's guide to refrigerated trailers

Typically, the transporting temperature for ambient and chilled loads is 37°F (3°C), and for frozen loads the transporting temperature is -4°F (-20°C).

Usually there are movable drop-down or slide curtains inside a refrigerated trailer to create two separate compartments. This makes it possible to have both an ambient and a frozen load on one trailer.

*Operation*

1. Flick the switch marked "start" or "run" from "off" to "start/run." Wait a few seconds. An alarm will sound, then the fridge will start up.

2. Use the switch or button marked "1" or "2" to select compartment 1 or 2, then press up/down arrows to alter the temperature and press the "=" button to confirm.

*Note: Some companies now use modern IntelliSet menu settings which relate to goods carried on a regular basis. Just select the product from the menu and the fridge will automatically adjust to the correct temperature.*

The diesel fuel tank is underslung beneath the trailer. An average tank holds 50 gallons. The fuel gauge is located on the side of the tank. Always check that the cap is tight and that the rubber seal is intact. One third to half a tank of fuel should usually see out a ten-hour shift.

*Fridge control panel*

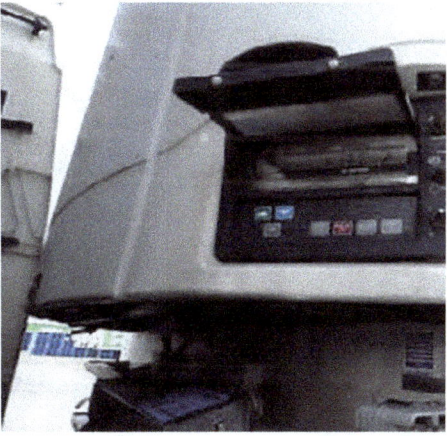

*Tri-axle fridge trailer (reefer)*

## Adjustable curtain systems

*Drop-down curtains*

*Side-slide curtains*

*Drop-down stowed curtain*

## User's guide to tautliners

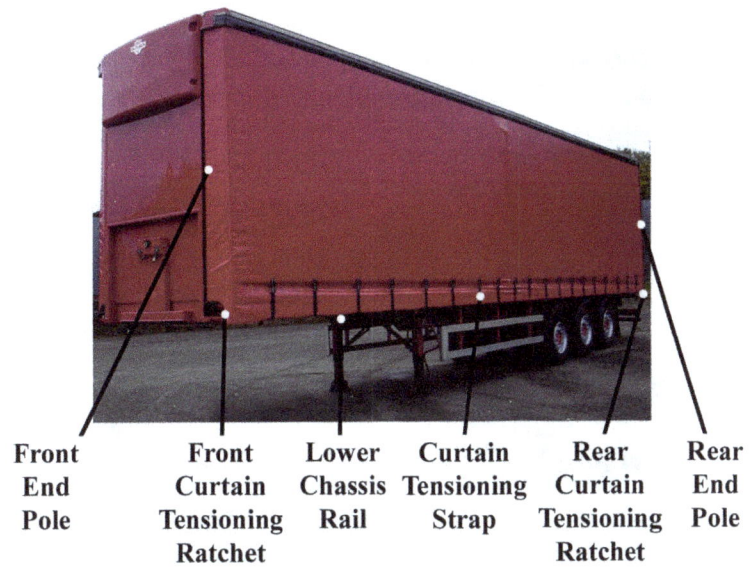

Front End Pole | Front Curtain Tensioning Ratchet | Lower Chassis Rail | Curtain Tensioning Strap | Rear Curtain Tensioning Ratchet | Rear End Pole

 Curtain tensioning strap. In this example, the strap is in the closed tense position. To release strap, lift lever [a], pull the rear strap down, and unhook [b] from lower chassis rail.

To secure the strap, pull the hook [b] under the lower chassis rail and secure to rail. Pull down on the upper strap until taut, and then pull down lever [a] until it clips into place.

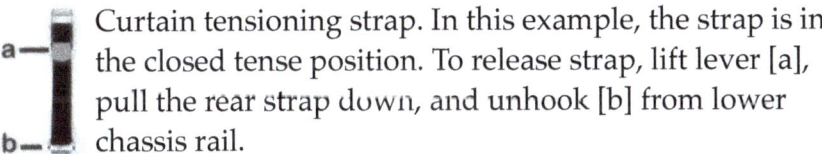 Typical corner tensioning ratchet. To release, push handle firmly inward. To tension, pull handle forward and backward until the curtain is tight.

### How to open the curtains

Release the curtain tensioning straps, as described above, to the extent you need to open the curtain. Next, release the corner tensioning ratchet and pull out the curtain attached to the corner pole. Push the pole upward until the bottom of the pole is free of the ratchet and pull outward. Lower the pole until it is free of the top securing pin. Pull the curtain back in the required direction.

**Warning:** *Never take out both corner poles at the same time. You risk pulling the curtain off the curtain rail, and it is very difficult to reattach.*

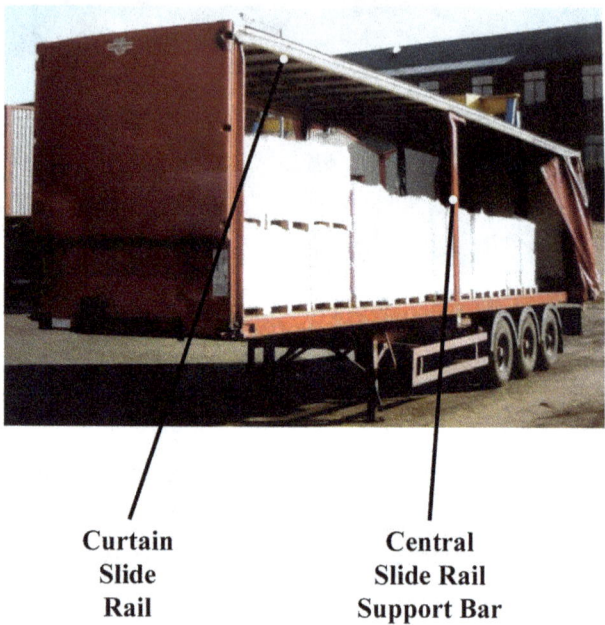

**Curtain Slide Rail**

**Central Slide Rail Support Bar**

### How to close the curtains

Pull the curtain closed and lift the top of the corner pole up until it is located in the top securing pin. Hold it up and locate the bottom of the pole onto ratchet. Use the ratchet to tension the curtain and then do up the curtain straps as previously described.

### Safety

When it is windy the curtains, strap hooks, and in particular the corner pole can flap about uncontrollably. This can result in serious injury or damage. To prevent this, it's best to only open the curtains to the minimum required. It's also advisable to pull the hooks up to release the lever and use the curtain strap nearest the curtain pole to clip it into place, either on the lower chassis rail or on one of the tensioned straps.

*Note:* The curtains are only there for the weatherproofing of the load. They are not rated for any load securement unless it's a heavy-duty trailer with planks or bars running along the sides

*Heavy duty curtain side trailer*

*Removable side planks, bars.
(Heavy items will still require chaining or strapping down to floor hoops fasteners. Planks and bars not overly strong).*

## Useful YouTube videos

- fftitrans, "Refrigeration Trailers — Proper Operation." youtube.com/watch?v=vBXH76zpXCI

- Bob Weaver, "Wickes IW Curtainsider V4." youtube.com/watch?v=OG4JgFD8PNo

Chapter **5**

# Safe Loading and Unloading

The aim of this chapter is to help you gain an understanding of the safe loading and unloading practices for van and reefer trailers. I have outlined the safe use and carriage of roller cages and pallets, and essential tips for the use of pump trucks. I have also included pictures and descriptions of how to use the most common height adjusters and tail lifts, and a list of considerations to keep in mind while you are loading/unloading.

As always there are many different types of equipment, but they all use the same basic principles.

For more information on loading, see chapter 6, "Load Securing."

## Roller cages

In the event of a full load of roller cages, you need to have a minimum of two load-restraining bars, one top, one bottom, spaced out evenly every five rows. If rollers are very heavy, e.g. on account of containing drinks, tins etc, you will need two bars every three rows. Pallets require two bars or straps every four or five rows.

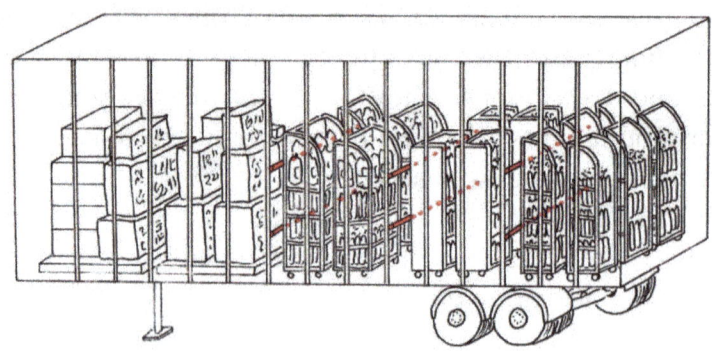

Beware taking the restraining bars off if the trailer is on a downhill incline. The bars could potentially be holding back three rows. If one or more rows start to move, you will not be able to **stop** them! You could be crushed inside the corner of the trailer, or the cages could fall off the back and hit someone.

*Correctly secured roller cages*

When unloading on an incline, if the vehicle is fitted with air suspension leveling systems, level the vehicle by raising or lowering the suspension on the truck or trailer, or both. Never remove straps or bars if the vehicle is not level. Each roller could easily weigh up to 700lb (around 300kg) each. This system applies to both semi and straight trucks.

*Suspension raised*  *Suspension lowered*

To adjust length prior to attaching or undoing a tightened ratchet strap, pull the clip back, then snap the handle back as far as it will go until it unlocks, releases and fully opens out. To tighten, pull clip back, close, then use the ratchet handle. Avoid twisting the strap. If it jams, it can be difficult to free up.

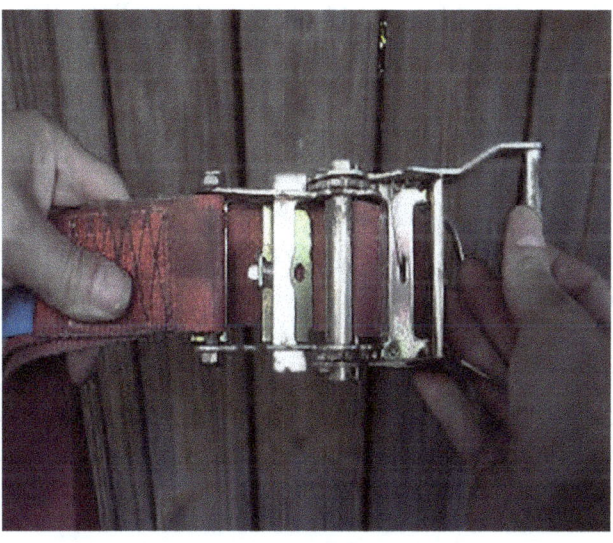

When manually handling full cages, always push or pull them. Don't walk alongside them. If full, they are heavy, and if a wheel breaks there is a high risk of physical injury to the shoulder or spine.

Empty rollers are designed to slot inside one another. The usual return loading system for a full load of empty rollers is to start at the front of the trailer, create three even forward-facing rows, then fit two restraining bars halfway along and two at the end of the rows.

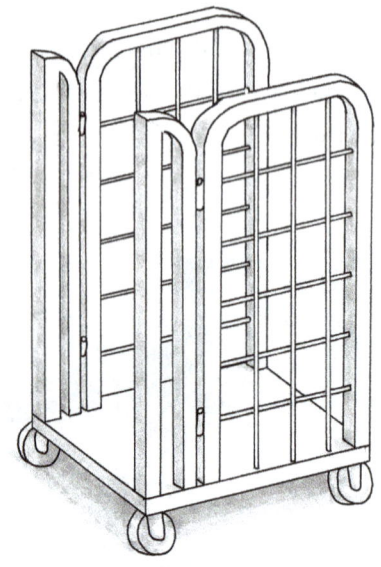

*Roller cage*

## Pump trucks

A pump truck acts as a manual version of a forklift. Its main purpose is loading and unloading pallets of goods. Pump the handle backward and forward to lift up the pallets. Press the handle/lever to lower.

If using a pump truck inside a trailer, you **must** ensure the vehicle is level. A pallet can easily weigh up to ten times a person's body weight. It can run away as you give chase down the trailer. Pump trucks often don't have brakes; the only way to stop them is by lowering the pallet.

Just remember to take it slow until you get used to using the pump truck. Be careful not to trap your feet under the wheels or pallet, or your hands between the pump truck handle and trailer side wall.

## Trailer height adjuster

The trailer height adjuster should be located on the outside rear corner of the trailer. You'll usually push it inward and then rotate the lever left or right to lower or raise it. Pull it back out until it clicks and it should self-level the trailer to the correct height.

## Truck height adjuster

The truck height adjuster is located either behind the driver's seat or on the side of the seat. The adjuster is simple to use.

Usually, you'll need to press the center of the switch until it illuminates, then press function arrows to raise or lower. Press the center of the switch again for the vehicle to self-level, i.e. return to normal operating height. When adjusting suspension height, either leave the control pad on the seat or write a note to self and put it on the dashboard. This acts as a reminder to prevent forgetting and driving away with the suspension airbags overinflated or underinflated. Driving away in the wrong position can cause damage to tires or suspension airbags.

## Tail lift operation

Some trucks have an isolator switch in the cab. This needs to be in the "on" position to operate the lift. Switches and buttons are usually found on the rear corner of the trailer, and there are usually more buttons just inside the trailer doors. A little lever clip will need to be pushed or pulled to unfold the lift.

> **Warning:** While raising the lift, there is a serious risk of **crushing your toes** if you get them trapped between the lift and the trailer floor. **Never put your hands in to try to free an underslung tail lift if it jams.** If it suddenly unjams it will crush your hands flat. Instead, get help or walk away. **Keep hands away from any moving parts!**

*Underslung tail lift and controls*     *Upright tail lift with load safety plates*

## Loading and unloading considerations

- Often, when changing between outside and inside tail lift operating buttons, an isolator switch next to the buttons has to be switched over. This is there to make sure only the driver has control over the lift. Remember to return the switch to outside buttons mode before closing the back doors.

- Leave sidelights switched on in the truck in order to be able to work interior trailer lights.

- When unloading or loading, put your safety first.

- Always check the load yourself and make sure it is fully secure. **Never** trust that someone else has chained, strapped or barred up the load properly. The loaders could have changed shift halfway, been distracted, been short of equipment or just not cared!

- Some trailers carry bars to hang clothes off. These are thin and lightweight; don't confuse them with heavy load-restraining bars!

- Try not to be hurried while loading or unloading. Again, your safety comes first, the load second.

- If for any reason you have to move the truck halfway through loading or unloading, stay calm and collected. Always, always resecure the load before moving. Remember, you are in the middle of a process, so retrace your previous steps when you return to the task.

## Useful YouTube videos

- Random stuff, "How to adjust the air suspension in scania truck." youtube.com/watch?v=P6abP2djvvc

- Pduesp, "How to adjust a semi trailer level suspension logistics DIY." youtube.com/watch?v=njY3Vsw-GhY

- S and E Logistics, "Tail lift." youtube.com/watch?v=butf9ThPBBU

- Alan White, "TAIL LIFT OPERATION." youtube.com/watch?v=3ahQLLKeUuQ

- Mathew Parry, "FRENNI TAIL LIFT TRAINING." youtube.com/watch?v=A4yWGTFo9mk

- Taylor Crane, "How to Use a Ratchet Strap to Secure a Load on a Trailer." youtube.com/watch?v=VWRcHawotr4

- DiscountRamps, "How To Use Ratchet Straps Like a Pro." youtube.com/watch?v=wDvTjzJ62Xs

- LGV Trainers, "Load securing Tensioning Bar." youtube.com/watch?v=iGQxswC8-yQ

- Junior Honduras, "Truck Driving | HOW TO INSTALL LOAD LOCKS/BARS and Securing Your Load." youtube.com/watch?v=2ND__RXckds

- Uline, "Load Bars." youtube.com/watch?v=mrv_oE8NAy8

SAFE LOADING AND UNLOADING

# Chapter 6

# Load Securing

This chapter contains information on personal safety, load safety, mandatory regulations, and how to use the different types of securing equipment.

For more information on load securing, see chapter 7, "Roping and Sheeting."

## The three types of load securement

### Fully contained

Cargo must not be able to shift or tip over and must be restrained from sideways movement by the vehicle structure, dunnage (loose wood, matting, or similar material used to keep cargo in position), or securing equipment.

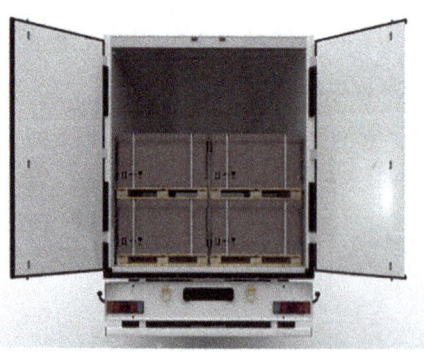

*Immobilized*

The cargo can be immobilized by structures or a combination of structures, bracing, and blocking.

*Secured on vehicle*

The cargo must be secured by tie-downs, which can be accompanied by bracing, blocking, friction mats, dunnage, other cargo, or a combination of all of these.

## Securement specifications

Each load will have its own securement specifications. Know what they are.

Questions to keep in mind:

- What is the load rating of the trailer?
- What is the weight of equipment being moved?

- How many straps or chains are needed?
- What are the load ratings of the chains, straps, and binders? These ratings can be found on the equipment by means of a stamp or fitted tag, or in the accompanying manuals.

## Equipment and working load limits

Each piece of equipment has a working load limit, or WLL. Here is a guide to the most commonly used transportation chains and straps.

### Chains

The most commonly used 3/8th chain is rated for 6,600lb (approximately 3,000kg) securement value if the number 7 appears on its markings. The marking could say "7," "rg 7," "L 7," "70" etc. This indicates it's a genuine type 70 chain. If there are no markings, the chain is automatically downrated to a smaller type 30, which has a much lower working load limit. Similarly, if a 5/8th chain is unmarked it too will be downrated and so on.

Always check chains are in good condition and have not been mended in the past. Things to look out for are stretched, bent, or twisted links, and welded or added lap or quick links. Any of the above make the chains void for use.

*Straps*

A marked or tagged three-inch strap has a WLL of 3,000lb (1,300kg).

A marked or tagged four-inch strap has a WLL of 4,000lb (1,800kg).

Some high-quality straps can exceed these limits. Check stamped-on markings or attached tags for the WLL.

Check for damage: rips, tears, holes. There should be little or none. The maximum damage allowed to the edge before a strap is void for use is:

- Half an inch for a three-inch strap.
- Three quarters of an inch for a four-inch strap.

## Official load strap down and weight regulations

LOAD SECURING

There must be a minimum of one strap secured every ten feet. If an article is over ten feet long, even by one inch, it will require an additional strap to stay within the length requirements. On an example load item that is 21 feet long, you would need three securing straps.

If the item is not placed up against the headboard, or in contact with the cargo in front of it, you will need to add at least one extra strap to stop forward or backward movement.

Tie-downs are required to secure at least half the weight of the article of cargo. For example, something weighing 20,000lb (9,000kg) would require a minimum of 10,000 pounds (4,500kg) WLL of cargo securement.

### Cross chaining, regulations and best practice for securing machinery

Keep the center of gravity as low as possible.

Equipment over 10,000lb (4,500kg), classed as heavy machinery, must have a minimum of four tie-downs. Any appendages require an extra tie-down.

There are two types of chain tighteners in use: ratchet binder and lever binder. These are also WLL rated and will be stamped with the working load limits.

*Procedure*

1. Find level ground.
2. Load machinery.
3. Unscrew ratchet binders full out.
4. Attach chains, pull tight.
5. If machine has manufacturers' tie-down points (eyelets), chain to these.
6. Set chains, two facing front, two facing back, creating opposite forward–backward forces. Set them on roughly 45-degree angles, creating downforce and preventing machinery from movement up, down, left, right, forward, or backward.

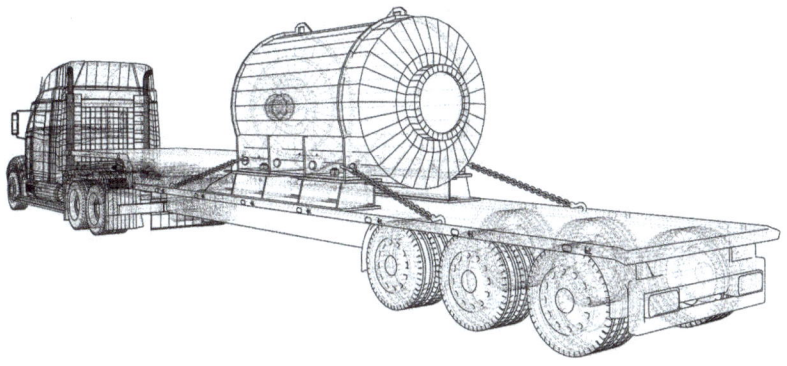

7. Attach binders and tighten chains evenly until taut.
8. Store any remainder of chain by wrapping it around binders.

Machinery with tires will be more difficult to secure tightly and likely to bounce slightly in transit, loosening chains. Check this type of load more often and be aware of slow punctures letting tires down, which will also loosen chains.

Beware of hydraulics. Hydraulics tend to creep down. **Never ever** get under raised hydraulics or in any tight space where machinery could creep, trap and potentially crush you to death.

Secure ratchet binders in fixed position to guard against them undoing in transit.

> *Note: See either FMSCA or CVSE websites for full individual American/Canadian load securement regulations.*

## Useful YouTube videos

- Keith Kalfas, "How To Use A Ratchet Strap the Ez way." youtube.com/watch?v=ucav1oA0kHA

- Choicemas, "Flatbed Securement, Lumber Load, Strapping, Elliottsburg PA." youtube.com/watch?v=zxrjqvxiv3I

- Christopher Leo Cox, "Load Securement demonstration." youtube.com/watch?v=w-qhcF7SrgE

- Rollin_18, "Strap setup." youtube.com/watch?v=eh4QeZLYLI8

# Chapter 7

# Roping and Sheeting

Explained below are the basics for the roping and sheeting (or tarping) of an open load.

Prior to attempting this task, you will need to undergo full training in the exact placing of sheets, straps, and ropes, and in the tying of the various knots used. Rest assured, you won't be expected to attempt any of these procedures until you have been shown by a professional.

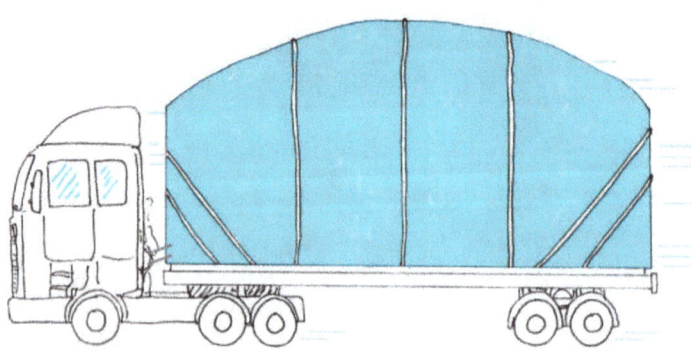

*Example A: Ropes not tight enough, tensioned unevenly*

*Example B: Sheets placed in wrong order*

## The basic principles of roping and sheeting

Ideally, you should find a quiet, sheltered part of the yard where you won't be disturbed or distracted.

Prior to fitting, add packing to prevent tarps from being damaged, padding around any sharp load edges.

### *To secure down a load using one sheet:*

Start at either end of the trailer. Roll the sheet out toward the opposite end of the trailer. When rolling the sheet out, be sure to keep it taut and to expel any trapped air as you go. Once the load is covered, secure all ropes and/or straps tightly, making sure they're all evenly tensioned.

### *To secure down a load using two sheets:*

Start at the rear end of the trailer. Attach the first sheet over the rear end of the trailer and roll it forward, then attach the second sheet over the front end of the trailer and roll it backward. Make sure that the front sheet overlaps with the rear sheet; this prevents the wind from getting underneath the rear sheet, which could loosen it and cause it to start to lift while in transit.

*Note: In windy conditions, you should only roll your sheeting out a little bit at a time and secure as you go.*

## Safety notes

- It's dangerous to walk on top of a load that's unstable and could move.

- It's also dangerous to walk on top of a load which has an unsecured sheet. You may fall down into a space in the load, or be blown off the top of the load when the wind lifts the sheet.

- In transit, friction from wood and especially metal loads can saw through tarps, straps, and ropes. Put packing on any sharp edges before placing the tarps and straps.

- Some loads will require strapping or chaining prior to tarping.

## Useful YouTube video

- Russell Worthing, "Sheeting a trailer." youtube.com/watch?v=wcHiXkwji-o

Chapter **8**

# Maneuvering

The aim of this chapter is to show you the recommended positioning techniques when maneuvering vehicles onto bays in busy yards. Two scenarios will be focused on:

- Maneuvering in a spacious yard.
- Maneuvering in a tight yard.

You should find this information useful, as you never know how much space you will be given. With practice, maneuvering becomes much easier.

### Maneuvering in a spacious yard

Drive along the rank until you reach the required bay. Swing the truck up toward the opposite row of bays. The idea here is to leave the trailer positioned toward the intended bay, making it easier to reverse in.

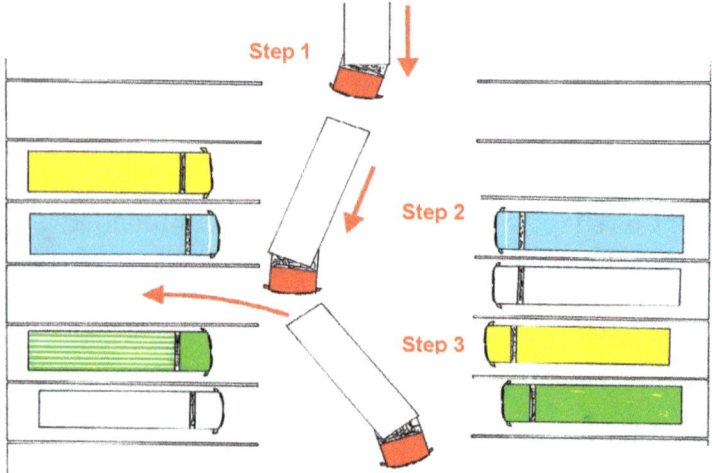

## Maneuvering in a tight/small yard

You need a different approach for a tight yard. Line up the back of the trailer with the intended bay, then jack-knife the trailer 180 degrees onto the bay. In tight yards, this maneuver is very difficult. If you need help, ask!

> *Note:* Raising the tractor second steer lift axle (if fitted) increases the turning circle. Sliding trailer tandem axles forward shortens the wheel base, enhancing maneuverability.

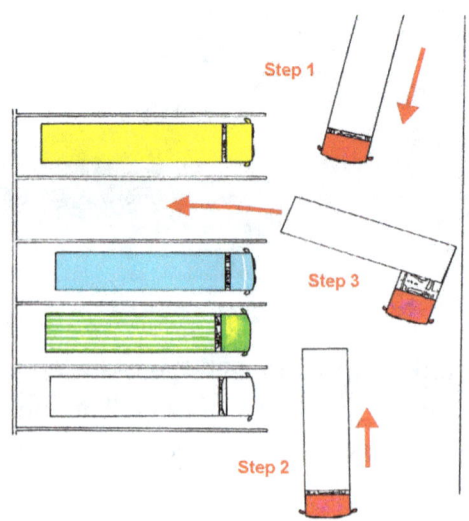

LOAD SECURING

# Chapter 9

## Key Safe: Lock on Dock

This chapter focuses on the key safe procedure. This system was designed to prevent accidents and injuries.

In the past, there were a lot of incidents in which trucks pulled off bays while loading or unloading was still taking place. This resulted in many injuries to loaders, some serious. For example, forklifts and pump trucks came crashing down off the docks.

Here are a couple of scenarios illustrating why, in the past, drivers have prematurely driven off:

- The driver fell asleep and woke up after some time to find that all was quiet. He/she looked at the time. Half asleep, he/she believed that unloading must have finished and so drove off.

- The driver could hear that loading was underway. He/she was under pressure to get to his/her next destination and therefore distracted. After a while, all went quiet. Not thinking clearly, he/she believed that loading had finished. Perhaps, due to past experience, he/she thought that there had been a change of shift in the warehouse and that the previous loader must have forgotten to change the bay light to green. He/she therefore drove off.

Please be aware that not all yards use the key safe procedure. In these situations, it is good to keep the above scenarios in mind while loading/unloading is taking place.

## Key safe (lock on dock) procedure

The usual procedure is to put the ignition keys onto a chain. The warehouse staff will pull them up and keep hold of them until the truck is loaded. Keep an eye on the mirror; on completion the bay light will change to green and the keys will be dropped.

If the keys are either hanging on the chain or in the truck, but the bay light is still on red:

- Go and speak to warehouse staff.
- Check all is fine.
- Get bay light changed to green.
- Drive off.

**Never** drive off on a red bay light!

## Picking up trailers (airline lock procedure)

- Check that bay light is on green.
- Reverse up to trailer.
- Fetch key from hook/chain next to building.
- Undo lock on airline (trailer).
- Put key and lock back on hook/chain.
- Commence coupling up to trailer.

## Dropping trailers

- Reverse trailer safely into empty bay.
- Uncouple truck from trailer.
- Fetch key and lock from hook/chain next to building.
- Secure lock to airline on trailer.
- Return key.
- Press button to change bay light to red.

## Safety notes

- Always check that the bay light is on green before attempting to couple up.
- **Never** reverse under a trailer on a red bay light.

*Note:* Don't forget to remove the trailer license plate when dropping trailer.

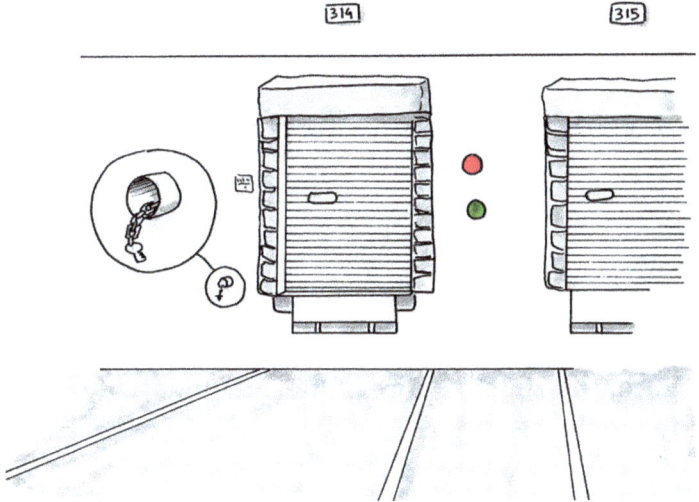

KEY SAFE: LOCK ON DOCK

Chapter **10**

# Environmentally Friendly Fuel-Saving Driving

Featured here are tips and techniques for driving a truck economically.

Nowadays, companies are very keen on this topic. This is hardly surprising, considering the price of fuel and the fact that an average fully loaded rig burns through a gallon of diesel every 6–9 miles (9–14 kilometers). Companies are therefore looking to all options to increase fuel economy.

In a successful attempt to cut costs, some larger companies (such as supermarkets) are now removing one of the two fitted fuel tanks and replacing it with a gas tank. Their trucks then run on dual fuel, which lowers fuel costs.

New fuel-efficient trucks have an added regen feature. Every so often the engine and exhaust system needs particulates such as soot cleared out through the exhaust. When the time is due, a sign or signs will appear on the dashboard. Full how-to directions for this procedure should be found inside the cab, sometimes on the back of the sun visor. When clearing the system, park a safe distance away from other vehicles.

*Eco-driving*

*LPG tank*

The following tips will help you to save as much fuel as possible:

Avoid unnecessary idling in cold weather if waiting to be loaded/unloaded. Switch off the engine and use night/bunk heater.

Adjust your driving style to one of forward thinking and anticipation. Try to keep up momentum. By reading the road ahead, it can be possible to see obstacles and hazards before reaching them, thus avoiding a lot of heavy braking and accelerating.

- Approach traffic lights gradually, avoiding (where possible) coming to a complete stop.

- Set your air deflector to correct height and angle.

- Change gear in the middle of the rev range.

- Check and correct all tire pressures.

- Avoid excessive speeding.

- Pull sheets/curtains on the trailer tight.

# Chapter 11

# Sliding Tandem Axles

Provided here is the recommended procedure to reset trailer axles. There are a few reasons you might need to do this:

- **Law.** Some states/provinces have unique regulation requirements pertaining to tandem axle placement lengths.
- **Weight.** Shifting load weight around, on and off tractor and trailer.
- **Maneuvering.** The further forward tandem axles are set, the tighter the turn the rig can execute.

## Sliding axles procedure

1. Park coupled-up rig on firm, level ground.
2. Apply park brake.
3. Lift and pull trailer adjusting locking pins lever(s); store in the locked-out position.
4. Visually check locking pins disengaged.
5. Return to tractor; apply trailer brake.
6. Disengage tractor brake.
7. To move axles back: select a low forward gear, crawl gently forward.
8. To move axles forward: select reverse.
9. Once axles are in desired place, apply park brake and trailer brake.
10. Release locking pins lever to engage pins.
11. Visually check pins located fully.
12. Return to tractor. Disengage park brake and, with trailer brake still applied, do a couple of short tug tests to firmly seat pins.
13. Inspect trailer airlines; make sure they are not trapped, too taut, or hanging down close to (or touching) road surface.

*Note:* *The pins locking lever is usually spring-loaded. If aligning locking pins is a struggle, release the lever, then steadily shunt forward and back until pins locate.*

## Weight transfer

Sliding tandems back allows weight to be transferred off the trailer onto the tractor, thus increasing drive (drive axle) and steer (steering axle) weights.

Sliding tandems forward allows weight to be transferred off the tractor onto the trailer, thus lowering drive and steer weights.

## Advice and safety notes

- If aligning tandems with a written mark or number on the trailer, take the center of the forward axle as the line-up point.
- Sliding axles can affect the headlights' aim.
- Placing axles forward increases back end trailer swing when cornering.

## Useful YouTube video

ataassociates1, "Sliding Tandem Axles." youtube.com/watch?v=vSa3HDE50R4

# Chapter 12

# Sliding Fifth Wheel

Provided here is a step-by-step guide to adjusting the fifth wheel position to comply with weight regulations and accommodate different types of trailer.

Again, there are several reasons you might want to do this:

- To make room for a freezer unit/axle weight transference on the tractor.

- Moving the fifth wheel back transfers weight off the steering axle(s) onto drives.

- Moving the fifth wheel forward transfers weight off the drive axle(s) onto steers.

## Sliding fifth wheel procedure

1. Park coupled-up rig on firm, level ground.
2. Apply park brake and trailer brake.
3. Set dashboard fifth wheel switch to release.
4. Release tractor brakes only.
5. Steadily shunt tractor back or forward to desired position.
6. Set dashboard fifth wheel switch to lock.
7. Take gentle tug test forward and back in order to seat locking pins.
8. Apply tractor brake.
9. Visually inspect to make sure fifth wheel pins are fully located.

## Advice

- Check that the clearance between the back of the cab and front (bulkhead) of the trailer is sufficient, allowing for full articulation turning of the rig without causing damage.
- Check airlines etc. are neither too taut or too loose. Overtightened airlines may snap during articulation turning. Airlines left hanging down are likely to get snagged and ripped out.

## Useful YouTube videos

- Junior Honduras, "Truck Driving – HOW to SLIDE your Fifth Wheel (5th Wheel) on the Truck." youtube.com/watch?v=6prjRvyYztw
- Smart Trucking, "How to Slide the Fifth Wheel on a Big Rig: Truck Driver Skills." youtube.com/watch?v=Noouxs2EG60

# Chapter 13

# User's Guide to Operating Trucks and Trailers

Presented in this chapter is a simple but comprehensive how-to guide to the operation of various vehicles.

Each description is split into three sections:

1. Operating procedures: a general overview of the vehicle and how to use it.
2. Specific hazards and problems to be aware of.
3. Personal safety risks and physical dangers involved in carrying out the job.

*Note: Many new vehicles have loading and unloading systems that can be operated either by levers or by remote control.*

## PTO (power take off)

In basic terms, the PTO is a large hydraulic pump which is powered by the truck engine and in turn powers all the ancillaries on the vehicle.

*To engage PTO (manual transmission)*

- Engine must be running.
- Press clutch to the floor.
- Turn the switch on.
- Release the clutch; a light will then illuminate to show the PTO is working.

*To engage PTO (automatic transmission)*

- Engine must be running.
- Gear stick placed in neutral position.
- Turn the switch on until it illuminates.

Turn the switch off to disengage before driving away. **It is not advisable to drive while the PTO is engaged.**

## Roll on, roll off/hook loader

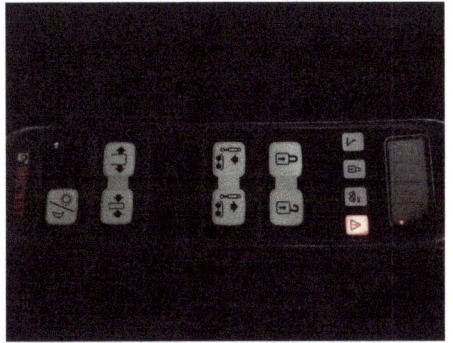

*Operating procedure: loading*

- Reverse up to the bin with the hook slightly lower than the bin's catch bar.
- Check the bin doors are closed.
- Engage PTO.
- Use joystick (if modern vehicle) or control pad (if older vehicle) to operate the hook and load bin onto vehicle.
- When it's fully on board, use the button marked "lock" to lock it into place.
- Reverse the procedure to unload bin.

*Operating procedure: tipping out the bin*

- Open and secure back doors. Leave the bin lock engaged to ensure bin is secured to truck.

- Use the joystick to lift the vehicle tipping ram.

**Note:** *Some new trucks have retractable rear bumpers; remember to retract before loading and unloading.*

*Hazards*

- Overhead wires pose a risk.

- Bowed back doors can allow the load (glass, timber) to shake out while driving.

- Weight of bins will be variable; beware of overloading.

- The height of bins also varies. With a large bin you may struggle to get under a 14'6" (4.5m) bridge. Always check total truck height.

- There's a risk of being hit by part of the load when opening doors.

- Wind catching the doors can cause them to swing uncontrollably.

- A top-heavy truck may roll over in transit.

## Skip truck

*Operating procedure: loading and unloading*

- Engage PTO.
- Lower stabilizers.
- Attach four chains.
- Sheet/unsheet the load.

*Operating procedure: tipping*

- Engage PTO.
- Attach four chains.
- Lower stabilizers.
- Lift up rear restraining bar.
- Slide skip back against restraining bar.
- Tilt skip upward to empty.

*Hazards*

- Always secure chains together when traveling without a skip on board. This is because chains are long and heavy and will swing out at the height of a pedestrian's head or a bus window!

- Watch out for falling debris while hoisting or unsheeting the skip.

- Be aware of the risk of being struck by another truck or machine when in a noisy, busy yard.

**Dump truck**

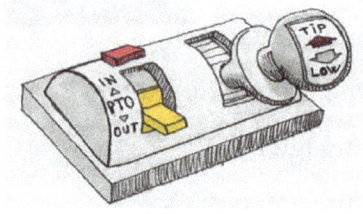

*Operating procedure*

- Find level ground prior to tipping.
- Remove load sheet and open tail board.
- Engage PTO. Pull lever back to raise body and forward to lower.

*Diff lock*

To be used in the event of the truck becoming stuck in mud. Engage the diff lock; this enables power supply to all the drive wheels simultaneously. The switch is found on the dashboard with an image of an axle on it.

**Note:** *The vehicle must be stationary before engaging the diff lock and it must be disengaged before the vehicle returns to road use.*

*Hazards*

- Overhead cables pose a risk.
- Stones may become wedged between tires and fly out under pressure, potentially smashing windshields of following vehicles.
- Punctures are a problem. Periodically kick the inner tires to see if they're sufficiently inflated
- Cuts and gashes in tire walls may render the tire illegal.
- Be careful not to drive off site with the tipper body still in raised position.
- The truck may roll over while tipping on uneven ground or in high winds, or if the load is frozen on one side inside the body.

## Grab truck

*Operating procedure: loading*

- Assess that the environment is safe. Check for pedestrians, overhead wires etc.

- Engage PTO.

- Lower stabilizers. Place blocks underneath to support stabilizers if the ground is very soft.

- Check the tailboard is closed.

- Use the levers located behind the cab, or the remote control pad (if in a new truck), to operate the grab.

*Operating procedure: tipping*

- Open tail board.

- Lift the grab off the load before tipping up.

All other details are the same as a tipper.

> *Note:* Most open loads require a covered sheet.
>
> Old-style traditional sheets are usually found stored rolled up on the top, at the front of the body. Simply unroll and secure ropes/straps to fixing points provided.
>
> New-style hydraulic easy sheets are very simple to use and no longer require the driver to climb up onto the load. Please note, many manufacturers have added a built-in failsafe to avoid damage. In these cases, none of the tipping controls will activate until the sheet and the mechanism are fully clear of the load.
> See harshequipment, "Harsh TL26NC Hookloader & Hydraulic Variwidth Sheet." youtube.com/watch?v=JuYz-SPqfbg

## Container truck (sea can)

*Operating procedure: loading*

Once the crane has finished its lift:

- Undo chains.
- Secure twist locks (locking container to trailer bed).
- Check container is thoroughly secure; check container security seal is in place.

## Operating procedure: unloading

- Make sure twist locks are fully undone. If not, the crane will lift container, truck, and trailer up into the air.

## Hazards

- Doors may open in transit.
- Top-heavy loads pose a hazard.
- Twist locks may jam; use a bar or hammer to free them up.
- Vehicle may roll over in transit due to top-heavy load while rounding tight bends.
- Opening container doors can be dangerous in a high wind.

**Note:** *Always look up to check the door locking bar mechanism has located properly at the top. This check is required for all vehicles fitted with barn doors.*

## Truck-mounted crane

Full training is necessary before use.

*Operating procedure*

- Assess environment.
- Find level ground.
- Engage PTO.
- Drop load-bearing stabilizer plates.
- Lower stabilizers.
- Adjust to level up the truck.
- Complete all crane checks.
- Check chains, shackles, and straps for defects, ensuring they meet regulations and are fit for the intended purpose.

*Hazards*

- Overhead wires pose a risk.
- Avoid overloading the crane.
- Stabilizers may sink into soft ground or through thin concrete.
- Chains or straps may break.
- High winds can cause load swinging issues.
- There is a danger of truck rollover due to overreaching with the crane, or stabilizers sinking into the ground.
- Mechanical failure can pose a risk to personal safety.
- Standing underneath a suspended load is dangerous. DON'T DO IT!!

## Low bed (low boy)

Full training is necessary before use.

*Goose neck*

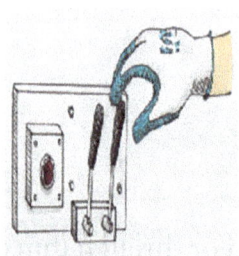

To simplify, there are two main types of trailer: goose neck and step frame.

### General overview of a goose neck trailer; training before use necessary

- The goose neck features a donkey engine which powers all hydraulics.
- You will need to be taught how to use the series of moveable pins and levers.
- The neck detaches fully from the rest of the trailer.

Loading takes place either from the front or over the side of the trailer. Other features include outriggers to extend the width of the bed.

*Operating procedure on a step frame*

*Step frame*

- Undo securing chains of the ramps.
- Lower and raise ramps by using twist knobs and levers located at the rear corner of the trailer.
- Loading takes place either from the back or over the side of the trailer. Other features include outriggers to extend the width of the bed.

*Hazards*

- Extreme height, length, or width of load can be hazardous. Check dimensions yourself; don't trust paperwork to be correct.
- Chains, tighteners, or straps may work loose in transit.
- Chains, tighteners, and straps may also break while being tensioned, potentially causing injury.
- There is a risk of tire blow-outs (due to heat build-up).
- Loads may slip off the trailer during loading and unloading, especially in icy conditions.
- Machinery with hydraulic components may creep down, causing a crush risk.

## Car transporter

Full training is necessary before use.

*Operating procedure*

- Unloading extend skids (ramps).
- Check car handbrake is on.
- Undo car wheel straps.
- Take out wheel chocks (wedges).
- Use operating levers to adjust decks.
- Drive cars off.
- Reverse procedure for unloading.

**Note:** *In the event of a full load, raise suspension before extending skids.*

*Hazards*

- Low bridges and trees pose a risk.
- High winds can also cause problems.
- There is a risk of hijacking.

## Drawbar combination

Full training is necessary before use.

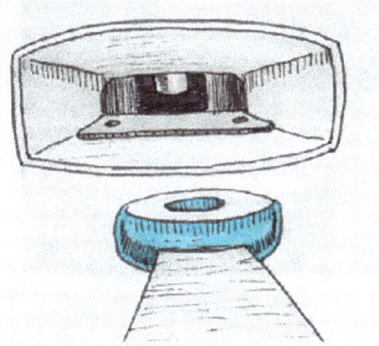

*Operating procedure*

Coupling involves basically the same principle as a semi truck and trailer combination, apart from the use of a drop-through locking pin mechanism. Always make sure the pin is locked in and the truck and trailer brakes are on before attaching airlines!

*Hazards*

- High winds.
- Tight yards.
- Reversing.
- A top-heavy load may cause the vehicle to roll over in transit.

**Note:** *Before going out for a job assessment on an unfamiliar vehicle, it is worth checking online to see if there is a video on it.*

Chapter **14**

# Department of Transportation (DOT) Weigh Stations

This chapter focuses on the mandatory weigh station procedures that all commercial drivers must adhere to.

## Terms used

**Maximum authorized mass** (MAM) means the weight of a vehicle or trailer including the maximum load that can be carried safely when it's being used on the road. This is also known as **gross vehicle weight** (GVW) or **permissible maximum weight**. It will be listed in the owner's manual and is normally shown on a plate or sticker fitted to the vehicle.

The plate or sticker may also show a **gross train weight** (GTW), also sometimes called **gross combination weight** (GCW). This is the total weight of the tractor unit plus trailer plus load.

The **unladen weight** of any vehicle is the weight of the vehicle when it's not carrying any passengers, goods, or other items. It includes the body and all parts normally used with the vehicle or trailer on a road. It doesn't include the weight of the fuel.

## Protocol

When approaching a weigh station on the highway there will be a notification sign. If a green light is showing, you can pass. With a red light or no light showing, you have to go in and scale unless the sign says the station is closed.

On entry, obey the slip road speed limits and any lane control signs.

On the scale, the vehicle gross weight and individual axle weights are assessed. You will then be informed, either by a green light or verbally, whether to report inside or to continue on your journey.

## Reasons you may be asked to report

- Truck suspected of being overweight.
- Paperwork check.
- Personal identification check.
- Log book/ELD inspection.
- Load inspection.
- Vehicle mechanical inspection.

Fines can be issued for faults with any of the above.

## Warning

If you blow by an open scale on a red light, it's likely DOT officials or even state troopers will come out, give chase, and issue a fine.

## Advice

- Know the specific gross weights and axle weights of the rig you are driving.
- If possible, weigh at the shipper.
- Weigh the rig yourself. Do not trust the shipper's paperwork; it may be incorrect.

*Note: For full in-depth dimensions and weights tables, go to the CVSE (Canada) or FMCSA (USA) websites.*

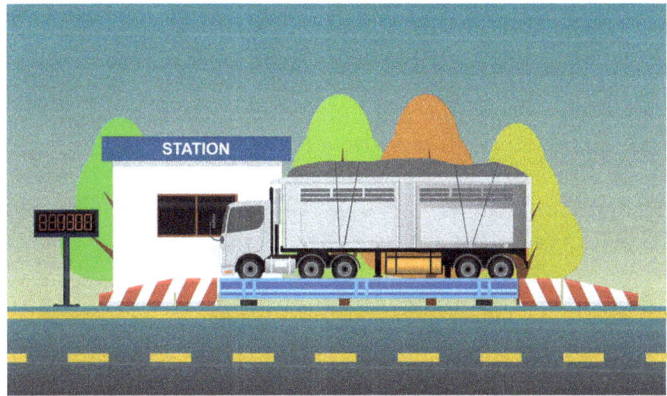

# Chapter 15

# Hours of Service

This chapter focuses on the mandatory drivers' hours of service regulations for both the United States and Canada.

## Hours of service regulations: United States of America

The following regulations apply to trucks, or truck and trailer combinations, that are for interstate commerce and:

- Weigh 10,001lb or more (including a load), or
- Have a gross weight rating or gross combination weight rating of 10,001lb or more, or
- Are transporting hazardous materials in a quantity requiring placards.

These rules are put in place for the safety of both CDL drivers and other road users. The regulations limit how much time can be spent driving in order to ensure drivers are rested.

There are federal hours of service regulations specific to different types of drivers; for example, those who carry property and those who carry passengers.

*Note: Drivers who transport property within a state are subject to state regulations but not federal regulations, whereas drivers who deliver materials from state to state must comply with federal regulations.*

## Drivers' hours: the basics

- Drivers may work no more than 60 hours on duty over seven consecutive days or 70 hours over eight days. They will need to keep a driver's log for seven days and eight days after, respectively.
- Every duty period must begin with at least ten hours off duty.
- Drivers may be on duty for a period of up to 14 hours following ten hours off duty, but they are limited to 11 hours of actual driving time.
- Drivers must take a mandatory 30-minute break by their eighth hour after coming on duty.
- The 14-hour duty period may not be extended with off-duty time for fuel stops, breaks etc.
- Optionally, if you've used up your hours, you may wish to reset. A reset occurs when a driver has taken 34 consecutive hours off duty. The work week starts after the last legal reset. For example, if you begin at 8 a.m. on Monday, then the work week continues until 8 a.m. the following Monday, unless you reset in that period.

In other words, you must keep to three maximum duty limits: the 14-hour driving window limit, the 11-hour active driving limit, and the seven-and-eight-day limits of 60 hours and 70 hours respectively.

## 14-hour driving window

> ***Example from FMCSA:*** *You have had 10 continuous hours off and you come to work at 6:00 a.m. You must not drive your truck after 8:00 p.m. that evening, which is 14 hours later. You may do other work after 8:00 p.m., but you cannot do any more driving until you have taken another 10 consecutive hours off, or the equivalent of at least 10 consecutive hours off duty.*

The 14-hour driving window is sometimes called a daily limit, though it's not directly based on a 24-hour period. The rules state you are allowed a period of 14 hours within which you can drive for up to 11 hours after being off duty for ten or more consecutive hours.

The driving window is limited to 14 consecutive hours driving even if you have taken some off-duty time during those 14 hours, e.g. a lunch break. During the 14-hour window the actual driving time allowance is 11 hours.

You are not allowed to drive if more than eight hours have elapsed since your last off-duty period of at least 30 minutes.

Once you have driven up to the daily limit of 11 hours, you must take ten or more consecutive hours off before driving again.

> ***Example from FMCSA:*** *You have had 10 consecutive hours off. You come to work at 6:00 a.m. and drive from 7:00 a.m. until 2:00 p.m. (7 hours driving). You take a 30-minute break as required, and then can drive for another 4 hours until 6:30 p.m. You must not drive again until you have at least 10 consecutive hours off duty. You may do other work after 6:30 p.m., but you cannot do any more driving of a commercial motor vehicle on a public road.*

## 30-minute rest break

Drivers are allowed to drive for eight hours after their last off-duty period of at least 30 minutes, bearing in mind the 11-hour maximum total driving time. For example:

- The driver could drive for 8 hours, take a half-hour break, then drive for a further 3 hours, totaling 11 hours.
- The driver could drive for 3 hours, take a half-hour break, then drive for a further 8 hours, totaling 11 hours.

It is worth knowing that drivers can work on past this eight-hour limit without taking the 30-minute break as long as they are not driving. This means that they can perform other on-duty, non-driving tasks (such as loading and unloading) more than eight hours after their last off-duty break, as long as they are not going over their total available on-duty hours determined by where they are operating.

Drivers who operate within 100 air miles of their normal work reporting location and satisfy the time limitations and record-keeping requirements are not subject to the 30-minute rest break requirement. This exception applies to any day in which a driver:

- Drives within a 100 air mile radius of their normal work reporting station,
- Returns to their work reporting location and is released within 12 consecutive hours, and
- Follows the 10-hour off-duty and 11-hour driving requirements for property-carrying commercial vehicles.

## 60/70-hour duty limit

> **Example from FMCSA:** *If you follow the 70-hour/8-day limit and work 14 hours per day for 5 days in a row, you will have been on duty for 70 hours. You would not be able to drive again until you drop below 70*

hours worked in an 8-day period. However, if your company allows you to use the 34-hour restart provision, you would have driving time available immediately after 34 consecutive hours off duty. You would then begin a new period of 8 consecutive days and have 70 hours available.

The 60/70-hour limit is based on a seven- or eight-day period, starting at the time specified by your motor carrier for the start of a 24 hour period.

The limit is sometimes thought of as a weekly limit. However, be aware this limit is not based on a set week, such as Sunday through Saturday. The limit is based on a rolling seven- or eight-day period. The oldest day's hours drop off at the end of each day when you calculate the total on-duty time for the past seven or eight days. For example, if you operate on a "70 hours per eight days" schedule, the current day would be the newest day of your eight-day period and the hours you worked nine days ago would drop out of the calculation.

**You are required to follow one of these two limits.**

If your company does not operate vehicles every day of the week, you are not allowed to drive a commercial motor vehicle after you've been on duty 60 hours during any seven consecutive days. Once you reach the 60-hour limit, you will not be able to drive a commercial motor vehicle again until you have dropped under 60 hours for the current period of seven consecutive days. You may do other work, but you are not allowed to do any more driving until you are off duty for long enough to get below the limit. Any other hours you work, whether they are for a motor carrier or someone else, must be added to the total.

If your company does operate vehicles every day of the week, your employer may assign you to the "70 hours per eight days" schedule. This means that you are not allowed to drive a commercial motor vehicle after you have been on duty for 70 hours in any eight consecutive days. Once you reach the 70-hour limit, you will not be able to drive again until you have dropped under 70 hours for the current period of eight consecutive days. You may do other work, but cannot do any more driving until you get below the limit. Any other hours you work, whether they are for a motor carrier or someone else, have to be added to the total.

*34-hour restart*

The hours of service regulations allow you to restart the 60- or 70-hour clock calculations by taking 34 or more consecutive hours off duty and/or in the sleeper berth. After you have taken at least 34 consecutive hours off duty, you have the full 60 or 70 hours available again. The use of a valid 34-hour restart resets a driver's weekly hours to zero.

*Adverse driving conditions exception*

If unexpected adverse driving conditions slow you down, you may drive up to two hours beyond the limit to complete what could have been driven in normal conditions. This means you could drive for up to 13 hours, which is two hours more than allowed under normal weather conditions. Adverse driving conditions mean things that you did not know about when you started your run, like snow, fog, or a shutdown of traffic due to an accident. Adverse driving conditions do not include situations that you should have known about, such as congested traffic during typical rush hour periods.

Even though you may drive two extra hours under this exception, you must not drive after the 14th consecutive hour after coming on duty, and you must comply with the minimum rest break provisions.

*16-hour short haul exception*

If you usually come back to your work-reporting location and go home at the end of your work day, you might be able to use the 16-hour short-haul exception. This exception allows you to extend the 14-consecutive-hour driving window to 16 hours once every seven consecutive days.

In order to use this exception, you must do the following:

- You must return to your work reporting location that day, as well as for your last five duty tours. A duty tour is the period of time from when you come to work to when you leave work, between your off-duty periods of at least ten consecutive hours.
- You must be released from duty within 16 hours after coming on duty.
- You must only use this exception once every seven consecutive days (unless you have taken 34 consecutive hours off to restart a seven/eight-day period).

## Hours of service regulations: Canada

The federal Canadian hours of service regulations apply to extra-provincial drivers (drivers operating in one or more province/territory and US drivers). In the commercial vehicle drivers' hours of service regulations, commercial vehicles are defined as trucks, tractors, trailers, or any combination of these, that have a gross vehicle weight exceeding 4,500kg. Buses with a seating capacity of more than ten persons, including the driver, are also considered commercial vehicles.

The regulations define two types of drivers: drivers travelling south of the 60th parallel and those driving north of the 60th parallel. The 60th parallel extends along the northern borders of British Columbia, Alberta, Saskatchewan, and Manitoba, and continues up through the furthest northern regions of Québec and Newfoundland/Labrador.

As most drivers come under the requirements for drivers south of the 60th parallel, the following information covers the regulations for those drivers. An explanation of the requirements for drivers north of the 60th parallel is also included in this chapter.

## Drivers' hours: the basics

- A "day" is defined as a 24-hour period that begins at the hour designated by the carrier.
- A "work shift" is defined as the total elapsed time between two off-duty periods of at least eight consecutive hours.
- Minimum of ten hours off duty every day.
- Maximum of 13 hours' driving in a day or work shift.
- No driving after 14 hours on duty in a day or work shift.
- No driving after 16 hours of total elapsed time in a work shift.

## Driver cycles

There are two cycles a driver must choose from. The cycles exist to limit the driver's on-duty time and to make sure the driver takes enough rest.

- Cycle 1 allows drivers to amass 70 hours of on-duty time over seven days.

- Cycle 2 allows drivers to amass 120 hours of on-duty time over 14 days. The driver must be off duty for at least 24 consecutive hours before accumulating any period of 70 on-duty hours.

If the driver works up to the 70-hour or 120-hour limit, they can reset the cycle by taking, respectively, 36 hours or 72 hours of off-duty time. Drivers can also change from cycle 1 to cycle 2 by taking 36 hours of off-duty time, or change from cycle 2 to cycle 1 by taking 72 hours of off-duty time.

All drivers, following any of the cycles, must have taken at least 24 continuous hours of off-duty time in any span of 14 days.

## Constraints

Drivers that are running south of the 60th parallel are subject to the following constraints for driving, on-duty time, and off-duty time:

- Drivers are not allowed to drive after amassing 13 hours' driving or 14 hours of on-duty time within a day.

- Drivers are required to take at least 10 hours of off-duty or sleeper berth time within a day. 2 hours of the total ten hours can be taken over the course of the day in blocks of no less than 30 minutes. These 2 hours must not be counted as part of a required 8-hour break. Take note, however, that the 2 additional hours can be added onto a required 8-hour break, thereby creating a consecutive 10-hour break.

- After a driver has amassed 13 hours' driving time or 14 hours' on-duty time, within a day or within their work shift, the driver must take a minimum of 8 hours off duty before commencing driving again.

## Duration of work shift and work shift limitations

Drivers are not allowed to drive after amassing 13 hours of driving or 14 hours of on-duty time within a shift. Drivers also cannot drive if over 16 hours have passed since the start of their work shift. The driver must take at least 8 consecutive hours off duty before the next work shift can begin. This means that drivers have 16 hours from the start of their shift to conclude all driving time, then park up.

## Deferring daily off-duty time

Sometimes, drivers may experience situations where they are not able to take the additional 2 hours of off-duty time in a day. The deferral provision allows a driver to defer up to 2 hours of the daily 10 hours' off-duty time to the next day. The deferral is allowed only if all of the following stipulations are adhered to:

- Total off-duty time taken over the 2 days is at least 20 hours.
- Off-duty time deferred is not part of a mandatory 8 continuous hours of off-duty time.
- Off-duty time that was deferred is added to the 8 continuous hours of off-duty time taken in the second day
- Total driving time over the two days is not greater than 26 hours.
- The driver makes a written entry in the remarks area of the log for each day to indicate whether they are operating on the first day or second day of the deferral.

## Splitting daily off-duty time

Solo drivers and team drivers driving commercial vehicles fitted with sleeper berths may split the daily off-duty time into two periods, as an alternative to taking one long period of off-duty time. Solo drivers who split time must adhere to the following;

- The total of the 2 periods of off-duty time is a minimum of ten hours.
- Each period of off-duty time is a minimum of 2 hours.
- Both periods of off-duty time are taken in the sleeper berth.
- No off-duty time is deferred to the next day.
- In the time prior to and following each period, there is no driving after 14 hours on duty.
- The driving time does not exceed 13 hours.
- The elapsed time does not include any driving after the 16th hour.

Team drivers, when splitting their daily off-duty time, must meet the same criteria as a single driver, with the exception that the periods of off-duty time taken must be a minimum of 4 hours and the total of the 2 periods of off-duty time must be at least 8 hours. Team drivers are still obliged to obtain 10 hours of off-duty time within a day.

In both a single driver and a team driver scenario, the driver(s) may not exceed 16 hours of elapsed time between the periods of off-duty time. Incorporated in the 16-hour elapsed time is all on-duty time, all off-duty time not taken in the sleeper berth, all periods of sleeper berth time that are less than 2 hours long (or 4 hours for team drivers), and any other period spent in the sleeper berth that fails to meet the requirements.

### Drivers north of the 60th parallel

The hours for operating a commercial vehicle north of the 60th parallel are more liberal than in the rest of Canada, with somewhat longer driving and elapsed time limits. This is helpful for drivers who work long hours in the summer and also for workers on the ice roads in the winter.

After amassing 15 hours' driving, or 18 hours of on-duty time, a driver north of the 60th parallel must take a minimum of eight hours off duty before commencing driving again. The daily off-duty time is reduced to eight hours off duty.

The rules prohibit drivers from driving after 20 hours have elapsed from the start of the work shift, i.e. the conclusion of the most recent period of eight or more hours off duty. The 20 hours consists of all driving, on-duty, and off-duty time between eight-hour off-duty periods.

Drivers north of the 60th parallel may split the required off-duty time in exactly the same way as drivers south of the 60th parallel. However, single drivers only need to attain eight hours, not ten hours, of off-duty time. Drivers north of the 60th parallel are also allowed 18 hours of elapsed time, instead of 16 hours, in the periods immediately prior to and after the periods of off-duty time.

The cycle limits for drivers north of the 60th parallel are:

- Cycle 1: 80 hours in seven days.
- Cycle 2: 120 hours in 14 days.

The cycle reset and switching provisions are the same as those for drivers south of the 60th parallel.

## Drivers' written paper log requirements, USA and Canada

The following information is required by law to be on a driver's log:

- Date.
- Start time if other than midnight.
- Driver's name, and, if applicable, co-driver's name.

- Driver's cycle.

- Start and ending odometer readings of all commercial vehicle operated by the driver.

- Name(s) and address(es) of the home terminal and principal place of business of every motor carrier by whom the driver was employed or otherwise engaged during the day.

- In the remarks area, a 14-day record of on-duty and off-duty time if no log was required the previous day.

- In the remarks area, if the driver is deferring time, an indication of whether the driver is operating under day 1 or day 2 of the deferral.

The driver is obliged to record the hours spent in each duty status on the graph grid and record the location of each duty status change. At the end of the day, the driver must record the total hours of each duty status, total distance driven during the day (minus personal use), and the ending odometer reading. The driver must also sign the log as a declaration of its accuracy.

### Electronic logging device (ELD)

An electronic logging device monitors a vehicle's engine to capture data on whether the engine is running, whether the vehicle is moving, miles driven, and duration of engine operation. The driver is required to manually update their duty activities throughout their shift. If you use an ELD, you do not have to keep a daily written paper log.

> **Note:** *Setting an alarm on your phone for 30 minutes before a statutory break must be taken can act as a useful reminder. This stops the break being forgotten and can be especially useful in busy cities where parking is at a premium.*

## Useful YouTube video

- MONROE CITY

  PeopleNet ELD How To Guide
  https:/youtube.com/watch?v=LtIbdw9rKLE

- Or go to FMCSA Or CVSE websites/ ELD user manual

# Chapter 16

# International Driving

Presented here is a brief overview of what it takes to be an international driver.

Planning skills are fundamental to the job and are required to achieve optimal time management, keeping to delivery schedules and remaining within the law.

## Essential daily considerations checklist

- Type of load to be carried.
- Load securing points.
- Type of trailer sufficient for outgoing and return load(s).
- Paperwork correct, permits supplied.
- Tarps supplied and in good condition.

- Weights, gross/axles.
- Chains, straps, binders: working load limit high enough to secure load(s).
- Province/state rules, weight limits, axle configuration differences.
- Setting tandem axles, according to weight distribution needed for load over axles.
- Setting fifth wheel, according to weight distribution needed for load over axles.
- Estimated time to delivery, taking into account the distance to be traveled and the speed the rig can travel at.
- Drivers' hours of service available, whether hours are sufficient for task, whether rest breaks will be needed on the way.
- Where/when to take mandatory breaks, where to get good food etc.
- Dates and best places to park up for a reset break.
- Shippers' opening hours and contact details; ring ahead to organize arrival time.
- Weather conditions, adverse conditions expected ahead affecting schedule.
- Temperature-controlled loads: full tank of fridge fuel, pre-check fridge functioning properly, check temperature remains constant on journey.
- City driving: estimate time of day entering urban areas (rush hours affect schedules).
- Fuel stops, locations, price, winter fuel quality, anti-gel.
- Accidents/road works ahead, delays.
- DOT scales, constant vehicle checks; keep it legal.

- Border controls, locations, correct paperwork.
- Pets' papers, vaccinations up to date.
- Time zones (may affect schedules).
- National holidays, country differences which affect shippers' closures.
- Parking availability.
- Hygiene: showers, washing clothes etc.
- Quality GPS.
- Maps, paper and/or electronic.
- Weight and scales apps.
- Truck stop apps.
- Tag, windshield bridge toll transponder fitted and working.
- Know vehicle gross and axle weights.

*Note: If your vehicle is at maximum weight with empty fuel tanks, refueling will push it over the limit. A hundred gallons (455 litres) will weigh approximately 700lb (300kg).*

- Know hours of service regulations for country, state, or province.
- Know speed limits for different states and provinces.
- Know the states and provinces in which winter tire chains are mandatory.
- Check tire chains are fully functioning and cam tool present.
- Check all tires have plenty of tread depth. Traveling long distances wears tires down quickly, especially with a heavy load and/or in hot conditions.
- Keep up-to-date vaccination certificates for any pets on board.

- Carry a first-aid kit, tools, spare bulbs and fuses, anti-gel, screen wash.
- Carry a high-quality sleeping bag in winter.

## Parking

Truck stops can often fill up during busy periods, making parking spaces hard to find. Here's some advice for parking up.

- Leave 30 minutes' driving time on the clock; this allows extra time to go and find somewhere else if the truck stop of choice is busy.
- Park early. The earlier you park, the more chance of finding a space.
- Download truck stop parking apps to find more options and locations.
- Reserve parking by app.
- Try to avoid parking next to a reefer trailer. If there is no choice, consider nosing into the parking spot. This at least gains you and your bed 50 feet of distance from the reefer motor.
- To avoid fatigue, keeping to some sort of regular routine is necessary.
- Earplugs are useful.
- On the edge of a big city or town, it is often safer for you and your load to park up at a truck stop rather than venture in hoping to find somewhere safe.

## Fuel

Here are a few fuel-related tips to bear in mind:

- Companies often take out individual deals with suppliers. Check which fuel stations your fuel card is accepted in.

- Rigs usually have dual tanks. In summer it's good practice not to go below a third of a tank, and in winter not below half. Fuel deliveries can sometimes be delayed due to bad weather or accidents, and severe weather can cause instantaneous road closures, resulting in you being stranded. No fuel means no heat!

- The fuel additive DEF is supplied at a separate pump. It has its own dashboard gauge and separate tank. The tank is often found around the tractor steps area, generally behind a panel.

## Cold conditions: tips and dangers

- Current American winter fuel will gel up in extreme temperatures. It is advisable to buy Canadian winter fuel when heading into the north.

- It's also advisable to add anti-gel to tanks when temperatures reach 0°F (-18°C) or below. Anti-gel lowers the freezing point of diesel. It is sold in bottles.

- Be aware that the strength and quality of anti-gel varies, and check reviews before buying. Read the label to make sure the anti-gel is designed to deal with the temperatures you expect to encounter.

- Temperatures in the north can reach -40°F (-40°C) and beyond. When traveling to the north, it is advisable to buy the super-strength anti-gels sold there.

*Note:* *When diesel fuel gels up, it blocks the fuel lines and filters, which in turn causes the engine to cut out. No fuel equals no engine and, crucially, no bunk heater. Temperatures as low as -20, -30, -40°C, or below 0°F, are a real and present threat to life! Plan ahead; don't get caught stranded in the middle of nowhere in a non-running truck!*

- If it's 5°F (-15°C) or below, try not to travel at night when there's no one around to help. Research and park only in places where there's 24-hour access to warm facilities.

- Keeping the fuel tanks full overnight helps to prevent freezing up.

- Prolonged use of the bunk heater may affect the batteries. It's a good idea to run the engine every 18 to 24 hours.

- For added safety, consider purchasing an extreme winter sleeping bag and scarf to keep with you. Ex-army sleeping bags can be found reasonably cheaply, but do check the quality.

- Brakes can freeze during extreme cold conditions. When the temperature hovers around the freezing point, moisture can also build up inside the brake lines and drums in the day, then freeze at night. To free off the brakes, try to tug the trailer forward and backward, pour a little ether into the lines, or climb underneath and hit the drums with a hammer.

*Note:* *For your safety, when climbing under a truck, always take the keys out of the ignition and be aware of anyone else around who may have spare keys.*

## Chapter 17

# Tire Chains

This chapter offers a simple guide to fitting single and double chains to the tractor axles.

### Fitting single chains to the lead drive axle

- Place a block of wood under inside of twin tire.

- Reverse up onto block. This lifts the whole of the outside tire completely off the ground, making access easy.

- Apply the handbrake, plus ideally block wheels to stop them moving.

- Lay chains stretched out with side fastening hooks facing upward.
- Check chains for broken links, broken cams, twists etc. Unfold to stretch out any twists.
- Fit chains over the outside tire with cams facing outward (toward you).
- Spread out evenly and semi-tight.
- Connect tightly, on inside of tire, the side fastenings, and then slide locking clips over.
- Connect tightly, on outside of tire, the side fastenings and cams.
- Tighten cam tensioners with cam tool. Go around the tire, tightening each a bit at a time, until all are evenly tensioned and chains are snugly tight.
- Take a short drive to settle chains, then if necessary retighten.

## Fitting double chains to the lead drive axle

This is a similar procedure to singles, but without having raised tires.

- Apply handbrake, plus ideally block wheels to stop them moving.
- Do chain checks.
- Fit chains evenly and tightly over leading drive axle twin tires.
- Tuck remainder of chain under bottom of tire, making sure side fastening hooks and cams are free and facing out. Avoid running over them.
- Drive forward by half a wheel rotation.
- Pull chains tight; attach inner and outer hooks as tightly as possible.
- Work around the wheel, tightening cams until evenly tensioned.
- Take a short drive. Retension any loose cams.
- Tuck in any loose chain links that could damage mudguards etc.

## Advice and safety notes

- Check the condition of chains and practice fitting them before winter comes around.
- Keep a head torch handy.
- The safe speed limit with chains fitted is around 30mph (50kmph).
- In icy conditions, try to be aware of passing traffic that could possibly lose control and slide toward you. As soon as possible, place your body either in front of or behind tires depending on which direction danger could come from. This way you should be able to see any unfolding accidents and get out of the way.

- *Always take keys out of the ignition if you are working around the wheels or under the truck. Be aware of anyone nearby who might have a spare set of keys.*

## Useful YouTube video

- Swift Academy
  Tire Chain tutorial
  https://www.youtube.com/watch?v=35pBbLWz0uY

- How to Install General Highway Service Semi Truck Tire Chains
  https://www.youtube.com/watch?v=TWmm2I5XypA

- Jason Woehier
  Chaining up
  https://www.youtube.com/channel/UCPmhrihpVoq2UNQiNp_1dJA

## Chapter 18

# Road Safety

Found here are notes on various hazards that are well worth taking the time to familiarize yourself with. A stitch in time saves nine.

- **Diff locks.** Engaged diff locks affect the steering. Only use at slow speeds and disengage before turning.
- **Fifth wheel malfunction.** Snow and ice picked up while bobtailing can on rare occasions compact in the jaws, affecting the kingpin's ability to lock on to a trailer. Clean out excess before coupling.
- **Jake brakes.** Jake brakes, also known as compression release engine brakes, are a useful addition to the overall braking system, especially on downhill inclines and when used in

conjunction with the foot brakes. They help to reduce some of the load on the brakes, resulting in less overheating and less brake fade.

Modern Jake brakes have variable strength settings. It is advisable to only use the highest settings in perfect weather conditions and the lowest settings in wet conditions, if at all.

The downside of a Jake brake is that it only slows the tractor, not the trailer. In dry conditions this is usually okay, but in wet and slippery conditions the added weight of the trailer's momentum can cause the tractor drives to lose traction, leading to loss of control and jack-knifing. When applying Jake brakes, the tractor drive axles should ideally be planted on solid dry road to cope with the weight of the trailer bearing down on them. Jack-knifing is caused by the trailer going faster than the tractor and essentially overwhelming it with the immensity of its weight. Ideally brake both tractor and trailer steadily in sync with each other.

*Note: When bobtailing, most of the weight of the vehicle is forward of all drive axles. Be very careful while cornering on icy wet roads and be very gentle if you use the Jake brake. Ideally don't.*

- **Cruise control.** Avoid using cruise control in adverse weather conditions. Cruise control delivers constant power to the drives and doesn't make any allowance for patches of ice etc.

- **Screen wash.** During winter, water and dirt kicked up off other vehicles can profoundly obscure visibility. Frozen windshield washers can lead very quickly to a complete inability to see. Keep plenty of screen wash in the truck.

- **Freezing rain.** Rain that falls and flash freezes on impact causes the road to turn into an ice rink. This is mainly a hazard in the north and also at altitude in the mountains. It's always worth looking at the weather forecast ahead. If there is a definite forecast of freezing rain, it is absolutely worth considering getting off the road and parking up. Better to be five minutes late in this life than five minutes early in the next.

- **Rock slides.** Rock slides most commonly occur on mountain canyon roads, especially at times of flood or spring thaw. The force of heavy rainwater running off the mountains can loosen and bring down rocks. Water expanding as it freezes and contracting as it thaws may also loosen and dislodge unstable rocks.

- **Temporary road works.** Be aware that some temporary road work sites do not have signs placed far enough back to give you sufficient, or even any, warning. During busy times, such as rush hour, traffic may be queuing way back beyond sight of the signs. Therefore, always ensure that you slow down when approaching a blind bend, because a fully laden rig will not be able to stop at a moment's notice. This is not an uncommon situation; you will come across this many times in the course of your career.

- **Tire scrub build-up.** During the hotter period of the year scrub builds up on the road surface. In itself, this is not a real problem until the first heavy rain shower, which turns it back into oil. Be ready for this hazard; the road can very suddenly turn into a skating ring. Heavy trucks slide easily. In fall, an added covering of wet leaves can make the road even more slippery; hit the brakes and the truck just slides.

- **Turning off the highway.** If you are planning to turn on to a slip road and your vision is obscured by another truck or bus in front, ensure you slow down in order to create space to see. There could potentially be a queue of traffic extending to the edge of the carriageway that you are not aware of.

- **Wasps, bees, and spiders.** Insects or spiders in the cab can be an instantaneous hazard. There are numerous accidents every year due to a driver's attention being diverted away from the road for a second or two. I've personally heard of at least one fatality. A passing car driver saw an oncoming truck driver doing battle with a bee. The truck veered off the road and hit a farm wall head-on.

- **Slamming into reverse.** Avoid stopping quickly and then instantly beginning to reverse. Give time for a possible cyclist or motorcyclist to take evasive action; they do not have a reverse gear and you will not hear them. I have seen a motorcyclist backpedaling a heavy bike for all he was worth, trying to get out of the way of a quickly reversing truck.

- **Blind spots and cyclists.** Cyclists and motorcyclists have a nasty habit of creeping up the inside of trucks undetected or stopping directly in front, below windshield level, at a set of traffic lights or junction. Be mindful of them getting their clothing or bag caught on the side of the truck and being dragged underneath. In the past there have been several very serious incidents where cyclists or motorcyclists have been sitting in the blind spots of truck mirrors. In a rush the truck driver suddenly changed their mind about which route to take. With or without indicating they turned suddenly, leaving no time for the cyclist or motorcyclist to react. You can guess the rest.

- **Black ice.** This is an unseen danger, especially found on untreated roads and shady areas after the temperature drops below freezing. I spoke to another semi driver who hit a stretch of black ice while driving at speed in the middle lane of a highway. The trailer started sliding side to side, pulling the tractor unit in and out of line: a precursor to jack-knifing. He managed to gently ease off the accelerator and slowly, as the speed decreased, it all came back under control and into line. He was fortunate.

- **Blinding low winter sun.** A real hazard, especially when cresting a hill while traveling toward the sun. Where safe to do so, if you can't see, slow down. Drive defensively to anticipate the sun's level. I know of a driver who crested a hill and was sun-blinded and completely unable to see anything for a few seconds. At the last moment, still partially blinded, he saw a queue of traffic. He swerved to avoid it and by doing so accidentally hit a lady walking her dog. The driver, subsequently traumatized, then faced charges for over two years until the case was finally dropped.

- **New trailers.** A brand-new truck or trailer can have a shiny, slippery floor, making for a much higher possibility of the load moving in transit. The load needs to be secured tightly to prevent the risk of truck rollover on tight bends.

- **Horses.** Horses are very easily spooked when they come into the proximity of a moving truck. Ideally pull over to the side of the road, switch off your engine and let them pass. If it's a tight space, very slowly crawl past them while looking for any possible signals from the rider to advance or stop and switch off.

- **Floods.** Extreme floods can wash away entire roads. If unsure of the road conditions ahead, radio other drivers to ensure the road is open and passable.

- **Wet brakes.** Always dry brakes out after driving through deep water. Do so by keeping your right foot on the accelerator, intermittently applying the brakes with the left foot. A few seconds at a time for a minute or so is all that's needed. Repeatedly doing this helps to expel any remaining water from the brake drums, and the friction heats up and dries out the brake shoes. Brakes are ineffective while wet. It's especially important to dry out brakes if the vehicle is loaded and you're planning to drive through a hilly area.

- **Oversize loads.** Obey pilot cars escorting oversize loads, especially in hilly areas. Look out for signals from the driver. Heavy loads need momentum to climb hills; grinding to a halt is not an option for them. They may become stuck on a hill, unable to gain the traction needed to get moving again. When traveling on single track roads, always wait for the lead pilot car to call you round before overtaking. Always make sure it's you they're calling round and that they're not beckoning another truck traveling in the opposite direction.

Don't be surprised by stones being flicked up at your windscreen from the oversize vehicle's tires if it moves over close or onto the verge to let you pass. Other possible hazards during overtaking include the oversize blowing a tire, tree branches being ripped down and ending up in your path, or strong side winds causing veering.

- **Map reading while driving.** It is obviously illegal and dangerous to map read while driving. Reading anything while driving is very distracting. The intention might be just to take a glance, but it is very easy to be drawn into the material you're looking at, and then find you traveled a fair distance down the road without paying attention.

- **Low bridges.** Always know the height of the vehicle you're traveling in and carry a tape measure. Similar-looking trailers can be deceptively different in height, so check for height markings written on. If none can be found, or if it's a flatbed load, measure it. It is not advised ever to trust measurements on any paperwork, or to fully trust a trucker's GPS. It is, however, very useful to carry an up-to-date trucker's atlas in the cab. With this it's possible to check all bridge heights to be encountered en route before traveling. On foggy, low-visibility days or at night, the last thing you want is to be approaching a bridge that can only be seen at the last minute, unsure if you can get under it.

- **Unplanned routes.** Accidents and road closures can cause an unforeseen diversion from a set route into unknown territory. This is much worse in foggy conditions or snow storms, where visibility is poor. If in doubt, pull over and check the map.

- **Top-heavy vehicles.** Some vehicles, due to their design and purpose, have a high center of gravity. This leaves them susceptible to potentially rolling over. One of the best examples of this is a hook loader (roll-on/roll-off). Caution should be taken when cornering with a fully loaded high bin on the back of one of these, especially if there's an adverse camber on the road. Always factor in potential hazards while cornering, such as blowing a tire, gusts of wind, adverse road cambers etc.

- **Wheel nuts working loose.** The nuts should be torqued up to the maximum specification. This is not always done! Do a visual check, then try at least three nuts on each wheel by hand. Over time, nuts that are not correctly torqued up can vibrate loose, leading to the wheel coming free and flying off the vehicle. The wheel then becomes an extremely heavy projectile bouncing along the road. Reasons why wheel nuts come loose include tire fitters being distracted or called away halfway through a job, wheels having been changed on the road in a hurry and/or without the correct tools etc.

- **Untested coupling.** When picking up a trailer, always carry out a tug test to make sure it's properly locked into the fifth wheel mechanism. After spending the night on the side of the road or at a truck stop, always complete a full tug test before moving away in the morning. This is to make sure no one has tampered with the mechanism during the night. It is very, very unusual, but it has happened in the past. I can only speculate on the sort of fool who would do this: perhaps a disgruntled ex-employee, or a person who's held on to their anger from a previous road rage incident.

- **Load shifting.** Frequently check loads that are open at the rear and consist of planks of wood, metal beams etc. While in transit, even if the load is secured down tightly, some central planks or beams may vibrate out backward and could end up on the road. This scenario is obviously not seen in the mirrors until too late. Metal sheeting and metal beams are some of the most awkward and easily lost loads. Metal on metal is never stable and always shifts a little.

*Note:* *Check a chained, strapped, or roped load after emergency braking, hitting a large bump, or hearing something unusual.*

- **Tire pressure or damage.** Avoid running on overinflated or underinflated tires. Doing so causes tires to wear down quickly or overheat, and increases the chances of a tire blowout. Prior to running, check tread depths and look for any damage such as cuts in the tread or sidewalls, cracks, or bulges. Checking the inside of a set of dual tires by sight is misleading; always hit or kick the tire to check it's properly inflated.

*Note:* *Uneven tread wear on the steer axle usually indicates the steering tracking is out of line and needs to be adjusted by a specialist.*

- **Road etiquette.** Give way on side roads etc. to trucks climbing up hills. This is good road manners and can be essential in wet, greasy, or icy conditions due to the climbing truck not being able to gain traction again once stopped.

- **Heat-induced slippery roads.** In extremely hot conditions the road surface can melt and the oil in the bitumen can bleed out onto the surface, leading to slippery conditions.

- **Becoming bogged.** Becoming wet or dry bogged is obviously something to be avoided. If you do have to park on a dubious verge, choose one that faces downhill and gives a slightly better chance of escape. Rocking the truck forward and backward, causing an ever-growing pendulum motion, can also aid escape. If all else fails, as a last throw of the dice, letting around a third to half of the air out of the drive tires can help. This creates a much larger tire footprint, which can make a huge difference in escaping a bog. It also works in snowy conditions.

- **Air leaks.** As part of standard vehicle checks or after coupling up to a trailer, switch off the engine and listen for air leaks. The usual culprits for air leaks are loose or split pipes, damaged diaphragms inside airbags, or failing brake boosters. Avoid driving with an air leak. It is illegal to drive with air leaks; the driver can be fined for doing so. Moreover, if the problem worsens, the truck will lose all of its air and all brakes will lock on, leaving it broken down and you possibly stranded. The most probable causes for picking up air leaks during a trip are becoming bogged, hitting debris, wildlife on the road or mechanical defects.

- **Suspended loads.** It is dangerous to stand under, or close to, a suspended load. The crane or forklift most likely uses hydraulics. On older equipment, if the hose breaks, the load will immediately and without warning come crashing down to the ground. The operator may be inexperienced or on their phone, and could move the wrong lever; a tire could blow on the loading machine; unforeseen gusts of wind could swing the load uncontrollably; chain, straps, or ropes could suddenly snap, or parts of the load could break free. Try to stand well clear of the load. Unexpected things do happen.

- **Tightening loads.** It is worth being aware in advance of possible failure of the straps, binders etc. Ratchets under force can break and suddenly spin loose. Lever binders can spring open when not fully snapped tight. In muddy or icy conditions, chains can slip easier, and so can you. It is very difficult, when applying maximum force to tightening devices, not to have all body weight directly over them. Be careful to stand as clear as possible of any device failure points. These items are solid and can give more than a bump on the head. Even newish tackle can fail; other drivers could potentially have abused it by overtightening it, hitting it with a hammer, or using it for a purpose it was never intended for, such as using a strap or chain to pull a truck out of a bog.

  Be careful when securing loads in busy yards or on the side of a road. Be aware of the traffic around you, especially when leaning back to apply full force. If the device slips or malfunctions it's possible to be knocked off balance and end up on your back three or four feet away from the load. Look for a break in the surrounding traffic before risking putting all your body weight into a securing device.

- **Suspension issues.** Blowing airbags or breaking springs can be caused by overloading, with excess weight stressing parts, plus a shock such as a bump or pothole in the road causing rupture, cracking, snapping etc. The suspension parts are vulnerable if shocked while under load and at an angle. Drive slowly and steadily over uneven ground. Blown airbags usually go off with a bang followed by a rush of air; broken springs often go with a bang or a cracking sound. Visually the vehicle will list lower on the side of the damaged parts. Vehicles shouldn't be driven with damaged suspension.

- **Tire changing.** When jacking up a vehicle on soft ground, soft tarmac or thin concrete, place a strong block or blocks underneath the axle to spread the weight. It is advisable to loosen the wheel nuts, then jack up the axle a few inches higher than the required height to remove the wheel. Now, wait a few minutes to see if the jack sinks before completely removing the wheel nuts and the wheel. Prepare the spare wheel in advance and have it close at hand, ready to be immediately fitted. The very last thing you want is to have to go under and re-jack up a sinking axle with no wheel on it. It's extremely dangerous, especially if it's a single axle, such as a steering axle. Ideally do not go underneath due to the potentially fatal crush risk. If you do decide to go under, throw the punctured wheel and any blocks under the center of the axle before climbing underneath.

*Note: Never trust a jack! It can slip out or creep down unseen if worn; the seals can rupture and the jack suddenly let go. Another vehicle can knock your vehicle off the jack. Unless the vehicle is firmly and safely blocked up, do not get any part of your body underneath the initial drop area.*

- **Dropping loaded trailers.** Assess the ground before uncoupling and dropping any trailer. On soft ground there is a possibility of the legs (landing gear) cracking and sinking down through thin concrete. On soft or wet ground, ideally place a large block of wood such as a railway sleeper underneath to support the legs. Also, when blocking the trailer wheels to stop them moving, chock the lead axle closest, because if the legs do sink the rear axle may lift up off the ground, leaving the block ineffective.

*Note: Be careful! In case of mechanical failure, do not climb under any unsupported, loaded trailer. The legs could malfunction and fail.*

## Chapter 19

# Driver Fatigue and Falling Asleep at the Wheel

Found here is an outline of the dangers of driver fatigue and some important advice for staying safe.

Be under no misapprehension; there is no definite, reliable sequence of events prior to falling asleep at the wheel. If you feel genuinely tired, pull over and take a break. **Do not** make the mistake of chancing it, pushing on through, relying on pulling over if the symptoms of drowsiness increase.

It's dangerous to wait until you notice signs such as; your eyelids becoming heavy, eyes constantly trying to close, head nodding down, difficulty in focusing, etc etc.

There is every chance you may well be sound asleep long before any secondary symptoms are experienced!.

## Serious fatigue symptoms!!

- Frequent blinking.
- Droopy eyelids.
- Difficulty focusing.
- Daydreaming.
- Scrambled thoughts.
- Missing exits and street signs.
- An inability to remember the last few miles driven.
- Constant yawning.
- Sore eyes.
- Head feeling heavy.
- Drifting across lanes, hitting the rumble strip of the shoulder.
- Suddenly being aware of getting too close to another vehicle.
- Feeling restless, irritable, confused.

## Ways to temporarily alleviate fatigue

- Open both windows and turn up the radio loud.
- Sugary foods and drinks containing caffeine.
- Pinch yourself to feel pain and **keep pinching** until you've pulled over.
- Say something out loud or sing.

If you are absolutely exhausted, you will have no control over falling asleep and no prior warning; it will just happen. **Pull over and stop!** Take a 20-minute sleep break, then get up and take a brisk walk. If you are still exhausted, sleep for another hour or two.

Sometimes you have to just give in to the situation. It is better to accept any potential repercussions for being late than to endanger yourself or an innocent family.

**Remember there are other people's lives in your hands, not just your own!**

# Chapter 20

# First Aid

This chapter is included in case of emergency. In your career as a driver, it is more than likely that you will come across incidents and accidents of various natures. It is well worth learning the first aid procedures outlined here, or at least having them to hand. To help an injured person or to save a life is a precious thing!

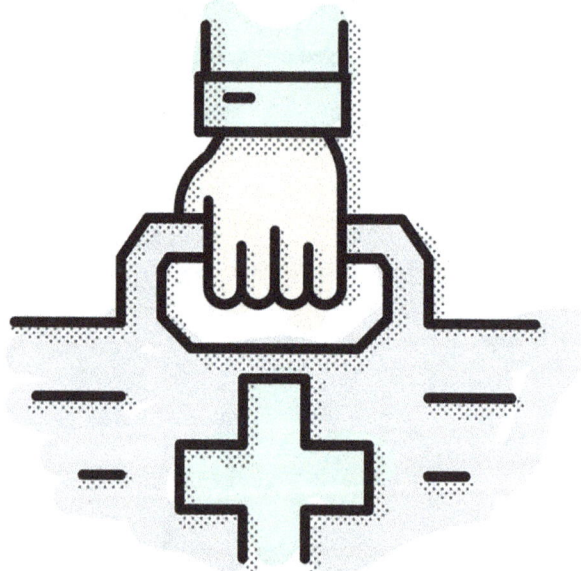

## Unconscious and breathing

When attending to a person who is unconscious, first make sure that their airway is opened up. Do this by gently tilting their head back with their chin pointing up, as shown in Fig. 1.

If you suspect an injury to the spine, don't tilt the neck; instead see "Spinal injuries," below.

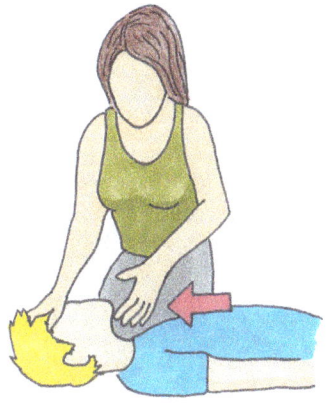

*Fig. 1*

Next, check that they are breathing normally. Watch for chest expansion and contraction and place your cheek by their mouth to feel for breaths, as shown in Fig. 2. Ideally do not take more than ten seconds to do this; time is of the utmost importance.

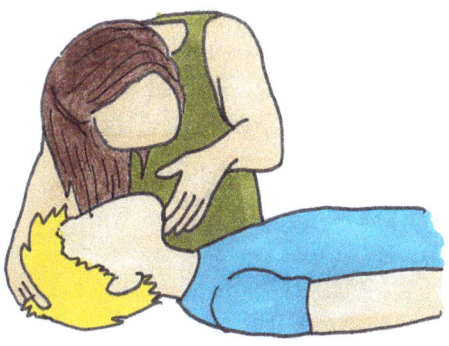

*Fig. 2*

If they are not breathing, call the emergency services and see "CPR: unconscious and not breathing," below.

If they are breathing, put them in the recovery position, unless you think their spine may be injured (see below). The recovery position, shown in Fig. 3, helps to prevent choking by keeping the airway open. It does this by allowing the patient's tongue to fall forward and any vomit or blood inside their mouth to drain out.

*Fig. 3*

Call the emergency services as soon as possible.

## Spinal injuries

If you judge that the person is suffering from an injury to the spine, ensure that their neck is kept as still as possible. Do not move or tilt their neck; instead use the jaw thrust technique as shown in Fig. 4. First, apply your hands to either side of their face. Next, use your fingertips to gently ease their jaw upwards. This will open up the airway, avoiding any movement of their neck.

*Fig. 4*

## CPR: unconscious and not breathing

As in the previous scenario, open up the person's airway by gently tilting their head backwards; see Fig. 1.

The next step is to check for signs of normal breathing. Check for chest expansion and contraction, then place your cheek next to their mouth to feel for the sensation of breaths, as shown in Fig. 2.

Having confirmed that they are not breathing, call the emergency services immediately. Alternatively, if there is another person at the scene, get them to call while you start cardiopulmonary resuscitation (CPR).

*Fig. 5*

CPR involves chest compressions and rescue breaths. It will keep blood circulating around a person's body, keeping their vital organs, including the brain, sustained and alive.

To perform chest compressions, lock your fingers together, as shown in Fig. 6. Keep the fingers of your lower hand straight and allow the fingers of your upper hand to wrap underneath your bottom hand, firmly holding your palm.

*Fig. 6*

Using the heel of your lower hand, apply pressure firmly downwards by 2–2.5in (5–6cm) in the centre of the chest; see Fig. 7. Make sure that you keep your arms straight while you are doing this.

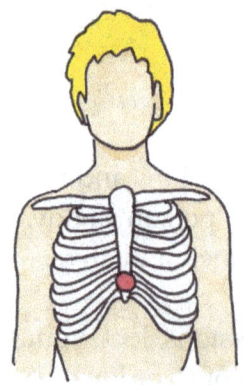

*Fig. 7*

Next, keeping your hands in position in the middle of their chest, cease applying pressure and allow the chest to return to its original position. You have now completed your first chest compression.

Repeatedly perform this technique at the rate of two compressions per second. Keep going until help arrives. If the patient starts breathing again, stop CPR and place them into the recovery position, as shown in Fig. 3.

If you are trained in CPR or feel confident and able with the technique, you should give two rescue breaths after completing 30 chest compressions and repeat.

## Administering rescue breaths

First, as in previous scenarios, make sure that the person's airway is open by tilting their head back, as shown in Fig. 1.

Next, pinch their nose firmly closed.

Take a deep breath and seal your mouth around theirs. Breathe into their mouth so as to make their chest rise.

Then detach your mouth so that the air can leave their chest. You will see when this happens as their chest will fall.

You have now performed one rescue breath. Repeat.

Keep repeating the whole routine, giving 30 chest compressions followed by two rescue breaths, until help arrives.

Again, if the patient starts breathing, stop CPR and place them into the recovery position, as shown in Fig. 3.

# Bleeding heavily

Heavy bleeding can be very upsetting. However, try to stay calm and in control. If a person's bleeding isn't stopped quickly, they may go into shock and lose consciousness, which can be a precursor to death.

Call the emergency services. Apply firm pressure on the wound with whatever you can find, such as a folded cloth or clean T-shirt, to stop or slow down the flow of blood.

*Fig. 8*

Your goal is to prevent the blood flowing out of the body. The pressure you apply will help the blood clot and stop the bleeding.

> **Note:** *If there's an object in the wound, do not remove it or press down directly onto it; this may cause added injury and pain. Instead, leave it in there and bandage around it.*
>
> *With any open wounds, there's a risk of infection transference; clean your hands and use gloves where possible.*

Next, while maintaining pressure on the wound, lift the part of the body that's bleeding well above the heart, as shown in Fig. 9. This will constrain the amount of blood flowing to the wound, slowing blood loss.

Keep pressure applied on the wound until help arrives.

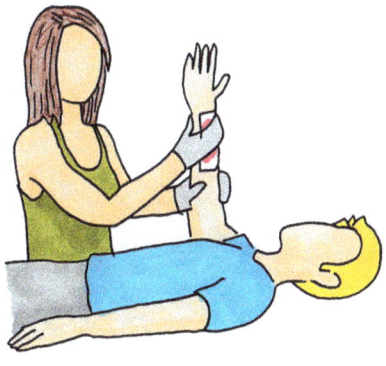

*Fig. 9*

If possible, place the patient in the shock treatment position: flat on their back with legs raised up. The goal is to have the legs higher up than the heart, increasing blood flow to the rest of their body. Support their raised legs with anything you have to hand, e.g. a jumper, coat, rucksack, blanket etc.

If they lose consciousness, see "Unconscious and breathing" or "CPR: unconscious and not breathing," above.

Always make sure that you call the emergency services as quickly as possible, or get another person to do it.

# A Note from the Author

First and formost, I would like to thank you for reading this book and wish you well on your journey into a new career! I do hope you have found this book accessible and informative, I've done my upmost to provide you with as much experiential knowledge and as many tools as possible to help in your success going forward.

I would like to state, this project is entirely self funded and published and relies solely on word of mouth. So if you feel this book has helped you, leaving an Amazon review or letting other drivers, driver forums, collegues etc know about it would be extremely helpful in raising awareness.

Further to this, if you have any ideas, topics that would help new drivers which you would like to see included in future editions, please feel free to email me at my writing email:

elite.publishing.services@gmail.com

Thank you and good luck!!

# Gallery

GALLERY

GALLERY

GALLERY

GALLERY

GALLERY

GALLERY

www.ingramcontent.com/pod-product-compliance
Lightning Source LLC
Chambersburg PA
CBHW070552160426
43199CB00014B/2476